What others are saying about *Therapeutic Astrology*

"A significant contribution to the emerging discipline of psychological astrology. Greg has masterfully shown how to integrate astrological and psychological theory in effective and responsible ways. A thought-provoking and much needed book."

Jonathan Tenney, M.A., MFCC, Astrologer, Psychotherapist

"A rare and excellent interdisciplinary work. This book provides a clear, comprehensive guide to the use of astrology as an immensely helpful counseling tool. Dr. Greg Bogart's profound understanding of both astrology and psychology and his years of practice as a counselor and teacher are evident throughout this book and its many remarkable case studies."

Shelley Jordan Montie, Astrologer

"I am convinced that astrology is a form of psychology, an enormously helpful technique for understanding life and mind. I am quite happy to see a professional psychotherapist who has investigated and worked with astrology in his counseling, and am sure that in the future we will see many others follow his courageous lead."

Zipporah Dobyns, Ph.D., Astrologer and Psychologist

"Bravo, Greg! After twenty years of practicing psychotherapy I've finally found someone who can articulate what's *really* going on in the psyche! This book is fascinating reading and a major contribution to professionals in both fields."

Dani Hart, M.A., Psychotherapist, Sound Mind Associates

Also by Greg Bogart

Astrology and Spiritual Awakening

Finding Your Life's Calling:
Spiritual Dimensions of Vocational Choice

Therapeutic Astrology

Using the Birth Chart in Psychotherapy
and Spiritual Counseling

Greg Bogart, Ph.D.

Dawn Mountain Press
Berkeley, CA

Therapeutic Astrology
by Greg Bogart

Published by
Dawn Mountain Press
P.O. Box 9563
Berkeley, CA 94709-0563
USA

Portions of this book previously appeared in the *Mountain Astrologer*, *The Astrotherapy Newsletter*, *NCGR Memberletter*, *Aspects*, and *The Astrological Journal*

Cover Design: Andrea DuFlon
Editor: Nancy Grimley Carleton
Proofreader: Diana Syverud

10 9 8 7 6 5 4 3 2 1
First Edition
Printed by McNaughton & Gunn, Saline, Michigan
Printed on acid-free, recycled paper

Library of Congress Catalog Card Number 95-83073
Bogart, Gregory C.
Therapeutic Astrology by Greg Bogart — 1st edition
1. Astrology 2. Psychology

ISBN # 0-9639068-6-0 (pbk.)

Contents

Acknowledgments

I would like to thank the following friends and colleagues for all of their support and sustainment: Rick Amaro, Mary Bartholomay, Ken Bowser, Linda Cogozzo, Sangye Drolma, Nur Gale, Dani Hart, Arthur Hastings, David Kesten, Colleen Mauro, Arlene Mazak, Barbara McEnerney, Charles Mintz, Barbara Morgan, Gayle Peterson, Meji Singh, Barbara Somerfield, Richard Tarnas, Tem Tarriktar, Jim Tucker, Chakrapani Ullal, and Bryan Wittine.

Many thanks to Zipporah Dobyns for her thoughtful feedback and many helpful suggestions. Thanks also to Demetra George for reviewing the manuscript and offering her comments. Thanks to Kate Sholly for some important editorial remarks. I am especially grateful to Nancy Grimley Carleton, Andrea DuFlon, and Diana Syverud. Without their friendly help this book could not have been completed.

I am indebted to each of the individuals whose stories are recounted here. All names have been changed and I have slightly altered certain details to preserve their anonymity.

A special thank you to Noel Tyl for his encouragement and incisive comments during the final stages of preparing this book for publication. Noel graciously took time out from his busy schedule to offer his assistance, which has been invaluable to me and for which I am deeply grateful.

Key To Symbols

Planets

☉ Sun
☽ Moon
☿ Mercury
♀ Venus
♂ Mars
♃ Jupiter
♄ Saturn
⚷ Chiron
♅ Uranus
♆ Neptune
♇ Pluto
☊ North Node
☋ South Node

Signs

♈ Aries
♉ Taurus
♊ Gemini
♋ Cancer
♌ Leo
♍ Virgo
♎ Libra
♏ Scorpio
♐ Sagittarius
♑ Capricorn
♒ Aquarius
♓ Pisces

Aspect Lines

———	180°	Opposition
— - — -	150°	Quincunx
— — —	135°	Sesquidradrate
———	120°	Trine
———	90°	Square
·············	60°	Sextile
———	45/30°	Semisquare/Semisextile

Houses

Astrology, a discipline rejected and ridiculed by Newtonian-Cartesian science, can prove of unusual value as a source of information about personality development and transformation. . . . For an approach that sees consciousness as a primary element of the universe that is woven into the very fabric of existence, and that recognizes archetypal structures as something that precedes and determines phenomena in the material world, the function of astrology would appear quite logical.

Stanislav Grof [1]

Astrology provides the best descriptions of character qualities. More than any other field, astrology gives background for the psychology of personality.

James Hillman [2]

Miss X was born in the first degrees of Cancer (actually about 3°). She knew her horoscope and was well aware of the significance of the moment of birth; she realized that the degree of the rising sign conditions the individuality of the horoscope. . . . Her horoscope shows four earth signs but no air sign. The danger coming from the animus is reflected in Moon Square Mercury.

I do not hesitate to take the synchronistic phenomena that underlie astrology seriously. Just as there is an eminently psychological reason for the existence of alchemy, so too in the case of astrology. Nowadays it is no longer interesting to know how far these two fields are aberrations; we should rather investigate the psychological foundations on which they rest.

Carl Jung [3]

Dedicated to my good friends

Jonathan Tenney
and
Shelley Jordan Montie

And to Diana Syverud
Who has brought so much joy into my life

Introduction

In recent decades there has been a growing interest in the psychological dimensions of astrology. This ancient discipline, once associated only with oracles and fortune telling, is now increasingly recognized as a potent and subtle language describing the internal dynamics of the psyche and the evolution of consciousness. Thanks largely to the illuminating work of writers such as Dane Rudhyar, Zipporah Dobyns, Noel Tyl, Liz Greene, Donna Cunningham, and Stephen Arroyo, we have come to understand the profound psychological significance of astrological symbols. This book examines one facet of this interface between astrology and psychology: the application of planetary symbolism in the context of psychotherapy. In these pages I record the results of my own work to integrate astrology — traditionally considered an esoteric metaphysical art — with efforts to assist acutely suffering individuals in the midst of complex personal transformations in the late twentieth century. My goal is to demonstrate how counselors can introduce astrology into their work, as well as to identify some of the difficulties involved in this endeavor.

This book contains three parts. Part I provides practical guidelines for the practice of therapeutic astrology, viewing the signs and houses of the birth chart as a template for identifying central counseling themes and issues. I discuss both the potentials and the contraindications of utilizing astrology in a therapeutic setting, as well as examining the broader issue of how disciplines as diverse as astrology and psychology can coexist and influence each other. Part II examines the planets as symbols of the central issues in human development that most counselors and therapists address in their work with clients. Part III looks at the question of how a transpersonal approach to astrology can assist individuals experiencing the upheavals of spiritual metamorphosis, as well as the significance of astrology for the field of transpersonal psychology. The many case examples presented throughout the book should be of special interest to professional therapists and counselors. Yet much of the material presented here will also be relevant to people who are using astrology as a form of *autotherapy,* or self-administered counseling, to guide themselves toward greater psychological and spiritual awareness.

This book focuses on the fundamentals of astrology: the ten major planets, zodiacal signs, houses, planetary aspects, transits and progressions. While Chapter Two briefly surveys the basics, if you are a complete beginner in the study of astrology I recommend that you also read some books that examine elementary material in a systematic way.[4] However, beyond knowledge of basic astrology, no specialized expertise is needed to understand this book. Rather than discussing many complicated astrological techniques, I prefer to focus on the most rudimentary symbols of the birth chart, which are so potent and meaningful that any counselor with knowledge of these principles can begin to apply them right away to work with clients.

I am often asked how I came to practice both astrology and psychotherapy. After I had studied astrology for a few years and began to interpret charts for other people, I noticed that I was exploring progressively deeper emotional issues and more intense kinds of psychological material. In fact, I found that people were entrusting me with the kinds of questions, dilemmas, and problems that they would ordinarily bring to a psychotherapist. I was also keenly aware that I lacked the knowledge to skillfully help people address such concerns as early emotional trauma, physical and sexual abuse, post-traumatic stress disorder, alcoholism and addiction, marital discord, and serious emotional disturbances such as major depression. I recognized that to deepen my work with others I needed further education. Thus, I returned to school for training as a psychotherapist.

However, as I practiced therapy for a while I realized that I could not divorce my efforts to help people in the role of a clinician from my work as an astrologer. I began to experiment with ways of using the information that an astrological chart provides to help me understand the client's inner dynamics, current life concerns, and the counseling process itself. The birth chart provides so many insights and can clarify the pertinent issues for a particular individual so vividly that I began to feel it was a great loss to practice psychotherapy without it. In short, I found astrology to be an essential counseling tool.

Over the years, I have met more and more therapists interested in learning about how astrology can be useful in their work. While some writers — most notably Donna Cunningham and Liz Greene — have previously discussed their use of the birth chart as a reference point for psychotherapy, I am not aware of any book that systematically examines many of the practical issues involved in the blending of astrology and psychotherapy. I have written *Therapeutic Astrology* to address this need.

Another question I am frequently asked is whether I use astrology with all of my clients or only some of them, and how I go about getting the client's birth information. The answer to the first question is no. For reasons that will become clear later, in some instances I feel it is not appropriate to broach the subject of astrology at all. The client's problems may be much better addressed through traditional counseling and therapeutic methods. At the same time, I may get the client's birth date from an intake form so that I can look up the positions of the natal planets in an ephemeris without necessarily mentioning it to the person. This never fails to give me useful insights. In other cases, I do a one-time chart reading to determine important themes in the person's life and use this as a starting point for the counseling process. Often I do not refer outwardly to the chart again after this initial session, but keep its symbolism in mind as I continue working with the client. In yet other instances, I use the birth chart in an ongoing way as a reference point during the course of therapy. It is through these kinds of explorations that I have arrived at the principles described in this book.

I am well aware that many of my colleagues in the field of psychology view astrology quite negatively. Indeed, as I will note in Chapter Four, many people in our scientifically oriented culture consider astrologers to be charlatans peddling regressive, deterministic, superstitious doctrines. I believe that in some isolated instances this description may hold true and that there are people who still utilize astrology in this manner. However, our understanding of the role of the astrologer has fundamentally changed in recent decades. Traditionally, an astrologer was a psychic who made pronouncements about the individual's destiny. But since the great modern astrologer Dane Rudhyar established a humanistic, person-centered approach to astrology,[5] more and more practitioners have begun to use the birth chart not as a predictive method but as a way of relating to a person — a person possessing the capacity for choice and the power to affect his or her destiny. There is a fundamental difference between the traditional astrology of prophecy or fortune telling and therapeutic astrology, which tries to strengthen our ability to direct our lives and author our own futures. Whereas historically astrology may have evoked fear and a sense of helplessness in the face of planetary influences, the goal of therapeutic astrology is to develop equanimity, freedom from fear, and the peace of mind that comes from understanding our place in the universe and the current challenges of our evolution. This book demonstrates how this remarkable celestial language, respected in many cultures of the past, can serve today as a valuable reference point for those seeking healing and personal transformation.

There are some types of psychotherapy that are primarily focused on symptom reduction through application of specific techniques, such as systematic desensitization for the treatment of phobias. But other approaches, generally known as the depth therapies, aim at addressing the client's total existential condition in a way that leads to a permanent change in outlook and behavior, an increase in energy, a better defined sense of purpose. There are numerous ingredients that contribute to such life changing therapy: the client's readiness to change; the counselor's empathy, ability to listen, and depth of experience and wisdom; good diagnosis and treatment planning; and a positive therapeutic alliance between counselor and client. All of these factors, among others, make possible effective therapeutic work. My personal testimony is that the responsible use of astrology is another factor that can help us to conduct transformative psychotherapy. The great psychologist Carl Jung knew this; he studied astrology and regularly examined the birth charts of his patients.[6]

Depth psychotherapy is not just the application of clinical techniques and the dispensing of advice. It is a ministry, an attending upon the soul of the client, one in which we become aware of, and attempt to cooperate with, the mysterious subterranean forces at work in the depths of the psyche. Most therapists have some awareness of how the unconscious leads us forward toward greater integration, revealing glimpses of our shadows and our as-yet unlived possibilities. Therapists are also aware that every case proceeds differently and that there is no one therapeutic outcome or course that is suitable for each client. Every person has to walk a different path and to actualize a distinctive set of potentials. Yet many therapists, while sensing the existence of these dimensions of their work, lack a framework that adequately organizes and deepens these kinds of perceptions.

The ancient and perennial art of astrology provides such a framework, revealing the person's internal dynamics and optimal developmental path. It is no less than a description of the rhythms of the universe and a map of the intrinsic wholeness of the individual. Reflection on the birth chart reveals an inner blueprint or a hidden architecture for each person's unfolding. It is also an incomparable means of understanding the tumultuous spiritual experiences that some of our clients report, experiences that traditional psychological training rarely prepares therapists to address.

Many therapists already use astrology with clients, quietly and behind the scenes. Unfortunately, most of us who do so feel we must hide this interest from our colleagues. It is only through recording detailed case histories of therapeutic work informed by celestial symbolism that we can demonstrate the value of the planetary perspective to the wider community of psychotherapists. That is the purpose of this book, which I hope will serve to introduce open-minded therapists, psychologists, pastoral counselors, and spiritual directors to the many powerful and practical insights that astrology has to offer.

PART I

The Practice of
Therapeutic Astrology

CHAPTER ONE

Using the Birth Chart in Psychotherapy

How can astrology aid a psychotherapist? The premise on which this book is based is that the study of astrology can greatly illuminate the process of psychotherapy — the most popular rite of passage for individuals in the contemporary Western world. In my own practice, I have found the astrological birth chart to be a useful reference point for initial assessment of clients, for understanding the changing seasons of the therapeutic relationship, and for discerning the approach to counseling that might be appropriate for a particular person.

This book describes how astrological symbols can be translated into the language of the therapeutic process. We will approach the use of astrology in the context of psychotherapy not so much as a way to predict events but as a means to help a person understand past or present developmental stresses (such as childhood trauma, financial difficulty, or marital crisis), to become centered in the present moment, and to make needed changes in attitudes and behaviors. In the practice of therapeutic astrology (which I sometimes refer to as "astrotherapy") we approach the chart with a growth-oriented attitude, assuming that every planetary position is purposeful and has positive potentials. We never want to disempower our clients or induce fear by stating that certain planetary placements are "bad," "weak," or "afflicted." We avoid reductionistic chart interpretations that will demean our clients, injure their hope or self-esteem, fill them with unrealistic expectations, or diminish their sense of open possibility for growth and change.

Utilizing a client's birth chart during the course of psychotherapy may be valuable for some of the following reasons:

- To identify major themes and repeated areas of emphasis in the person's life.
- To perceive unconscious patterns of thought, feeling, or behavior.
- To help the counselor understand the client more fully and thereby increase therapeutic empathy.
- To help the client view life from a symbolic and cyclic perspective that reveals the underlying meaning and purpose of events, including chaotic or painful experiences.
- To facilitate the therapist's ability to help the client resolve core life dilemmas and navigate crucial transition periods.
- To explore the kinds of experiences the client might expect during a given period of time, as indicated by planetary transits and progressions.

- To help the client make choices that are appropriate to the developmental path suggested by the birth chart.
- To understand the rhythm and various stages of psycho-therapy and processes such as resistance, decompensation, transference, and counter-transference.[7]
- To assist clients through crises of spiritual awakening.

This last point is particularly important, for many therapists do not understand how to respond to the yearnings of clients for expansion and metamorphosis beyond the ego, beyond the stages of adaptation to society. As we will see later in this book, astrology provides a map of the complete course of human evolution, including the transpersonal dimensions so often ignored in traditional psychotherapy.

Astrology teaches us that life constantly offers us new chances for renewal; we can always move forward from where we are. Throughout this book we will see how study of the stellar art can help us find the next steps we need to take, steps toward improvement, growth, and progress. Many case examples illustrate the fact that as we take these steps and learn to act with a more conscious sense of purpose, our deepest inner sufferings diminish. Synchronizing our lives with the planetary pattern moves us rapidly forward in our evolution. It is a safe, effective way of identifying and addressing our current developmental needs, and mastering the lessons that life presents to us. It teaches us to find meaning in our struggles, and gives us faith that we can overcome them as we strive to meet our goals. In the next chapter we begin our exploration of therapeutic astrology by building a foundation in the most fundamental celestial symbols.

CHAPTER TWO

Reviewing the Basics

A natal chart depicts the positions of the major planets of our
solar system at the moment of birth. It represents our
potentials, dominant character traits and interests, and the
steps we need to take to actualize our potentials and to grow
toward greater maturity and awareness. The chart contains four
central components: planets, signs, houses, and aspects. Planets,
signs, and houses represent archetypal characters, themes, and
situations that all of us face to some degree in the course of
life. Yet their unique arrangement in the birth map indicates
which of these archetypal structures or themes are emphasized
in the person's life. We also gain insight into how the
potentials depicted in the birth chart come to fruition over
time through the study of transits and progressions. This
chapter briefly introduces these central components of the

birth chart. In subsequent chapters we learn to interpret them specifically in the context of the therapeutic process.

The Planets

The planets represent ten facets of personality, each of which we must awaken, express, and embody in order to become complete human beings. The Sun represents the ego, our conscious identity and sense of specialness and unique self-hood; it is the joy, centeredness, and radiance that only comes from knowing who we are. The Moon symbolizes our unconscious moods and reactions, inner needs, and prevailing emotional states. Mercury symbolizes our way of thinking, learning, and speaking. Venus signifies our way of relating to others, our tastes and sense of beauty, and our desire for pleasure. Mars represents our way of asserting ourselves, taking the initiative, and expressing our desires and sexual drives. Jupiter symbolizes our goals and social aspirations, and our desire for a philosophically meaningful existence. Saturn sym-bolizes our desire for security and accomplishment, and areas where hard work, responsibility, commitments, and disci-plined effort are necessary. Saturn also indicates problematic areas of life that may require focused, persistent work to develop greater confidence and strength.

Having met the challenges of maturation and social adaptation symbolized by Saturn, the outer planets (Uranus, Neptune, and Pluto) direct our attention to further stages of evolution in which we become more than just socially adjusted individuals. Uranus awakens in us the desire for liberation from cultural norms and the realization that we are free to live and express ourselves in unique or unconventional ways. Uranus often manifests as a defiant attitude, restless experimentation, and a desire to reform society. Neptune represents our spirituality, our urge to experience subtle, non-physical dimensions of existence, through imagination, religious faith, dreams, psychic perceptions, and mystical experiences. It governs states of confusion, uncertainty, disorientation, and disability, as well as drugs, alcohol, and addictions. Finally, Pluto represents the experience of crisis and renewal, and the emergence into awareness of anything we have repressed. Pluto also teaches us about the appropriate use of our personal powers and capacities through facing the negative effects of cruelty, violence, or dictatorial power. Uranus, Neptune, and Pluto represent stages of development that are not addressed by most psychotherapies, with the exception of those informed by a transpersonal perspective (the topic of discussion in Chapters Ten and Eleven).

The Signs of the Zodiac

The planets appear (from our earth-centered perspective) to revolve around the Earth. We measure the position of the planets at any time along the plane of the ecliptic, the path of the Sun's apparent motion around the Earth. (In actuality, the Earth revolves around the Sun.) The circle of the ecliptic is divided into twelve sections, comprising thirty degrees of arc each, known as the *signs of the zodiac*. As each planet passes through these signs, its style of expressing its basic nature (for example: Moon, to feel; Mars, to act) changes. Each sign represents a set of essential human concerns:

- Aries (ruled by Mars): energy, desire, aggression, and competitiveness; awareness of oneself as a distinctive person; self-centered attitudes.
- Taurus (ruled by Venus): groundedness, ease, material stability, money, possessions, sensuality.
- Gemini (ruled by Mercury): mental activity, curiosity, learning, thinking, and speaking.
- Cancer (ruled by Moon): feelings, memory, home and family; nurturing of self and others; emotional bonding.
- Leo (ruled by Sun): self-expression, play, pride, dignity, the expression of love; dramatic display of the self.
- Virgo (ruled by Mercury): self-improvement, concerns about health, diet, and employment.
- Libra (ruled by Venus): relationship, cooperation, harmony, beauty, and balance; deference to others.
- Scorpio (co-ruled by Pluto and Mars): interpersonal struggle, sexuality, sharing of resources; awareness of our mortality.
- Sagittarius (ruled by Jupiter): the search for truth, meaning, religious or moral principles; travel and education.
- Capricorn (ruled by Saturn): career, professional goals and achievements, concern with social position and status; conformity to tradition.
- Aquarius (ruled by Uranus): political awareness, involvement with groups, revolution, reform or defiance of tradition.
- Pisces (ruled by Neptune): self-transcendence; expanded consciousness, inner vision, compassion, altruism.

Each planet is said to be the ruler of one or two signs. That is, this planet has a particular affinity with that sign and is at home there. This planet is also known as the *dispositor* of that sign and of any other planets placed there.

Aspects

Planets constantly interrelate with other planets as they transit through the sky, forming *aspects* when they reach important geometric relationships with one another. When two planets are near each other in the sky they are said to be in *conjunction*, and when they are 180° apart they are said to be in *opposition*. When two planets are 90° apart they are said to be *square* to one another. A 60° aspect is called a *sextile*, while an aspect of 120° is called a *trine*. Two planets separated by 150° are said to be in a *quincunx* aspect. While there are other angular relationships between planets that define aspects (such as the 45° semi-square and the 135° sesquiquadrate), these are the most important ones, the ones most likely to clearly impact our lives. These are the aspects I will mention in this book.[8]

Traditional astrological doctrines stated that certain aspects such as the trine and sextile are good, easy, and beneficent, while others such as the square, opposition, and quincunx are bad, difficult, and malefic in influence. These black and white distinctions have been reevaluated in recent years, as we have come to recognize that trines and sextiles are not always "good" and that squares and oppositions are not inherently malefic. Yet there is some agreement among most astrologers that sextile and trine aspects represent natural talents, opportunities, and easy, almost effortless blendings of the two planetary energies. The conjunction is neutral, its nature being determined by the qualities of the two planets involved. A conjunction represents a need to blend the functioning of two planets so they operate as a single, integrated unit. Some planetary pairs can achieve this blending more easily than others. A Venus-Moon conjunction tends to be a very soft, warm planetary contact, while a conjunction of Mars and Uranus can be highly volatile.

The square, opposition, and quincunx, on the other hand, are believed to represent more stressful, challenging relationships between planets that at times operate discordantly, in a way that creates some friction in the person's life. For example, a man with Jupiter in the 7th house (relationships) square Saturn in the 4th house (family) experienced some stress because his parents did not approve of his friends or his choice of marital partner. A woman with Mercury-Neptune quincunx Saturn was intensely committed to becoming a poet (Mercury-Neptune) yet experienced inner tension because material pressures and her work schedule (Saturn) made it difficult to find time to write.

It is important to recognize that aspects such as the square, opposition, and quincunx are not "bad." Quite to the contrary, these are the planetary interactions that stimulate us to change and therefore are responsible for much of our growth in functioning and awareness. Nearly every chart has some mixture of "easy," harmonious aspects and "difficult," stressful aspects.

There are increasing numbers of astrologers who view the specific aspect as less important than the nature of the two planets that are interacting. For example, a person with any contact of Mercury and Neptune, be it conjunction, square, or

trine, will tend to be interested in imaginative thinking and ☿/♃
writing, while any Mars-Pluto aspect gives a certain physical ♂/♇
vigor, strength, and powerful assertiveness. In this view, all
aspects represent a synergistic connection between the planets.
The planetary pair involved is thus seen as more important
than the specific aspect. The reader will see this perspective
reflected in my approach to aspects in this book.

The Houses

At the birth moment each of the planets is placed in one of the
twelve houses of the birth chart. Houses are areas of the sky that
are defined by dividing up the sky at any moment (such as the
moment of a person's birth) into twelve sections. Using the
exact date, place, and time of birth, an astrologer determines
the position of the point directly overhead (the "Midheaven"
or "MC"), the point opposite the MC (the "IC," or "*imum
coeli*," the bottom of the sky), the point on the Eastern horizon
(the "Ascendant") and the point on the Western horizon (the
"Descendant"). The Ascendant (cusp of the 1st house) marks
the person's appearance and behaviors that are immediately
apparent to others. While it doesn't tell us about the essence of
the person, it tells us about how the person looks, acts, and
perceives himself. The Descendant (cusp of the 7th house)
provides initial indications of the kinds of friends, spouses,
and partners that a person will tend to attract, as well as a
basic way of meeting the challenge of relationships with
others. The IC (cusp of the 4th house) represents our sense of
roots and our desire to establish a stable foundation for our
personal lives through home, family, and connection to a

specific place or nation. The MC (cusp of the 10th house) represents the way we envision ourselves blossoming into the world, the position we hold in society, and the career we pursue. These four angles define four quadrants of the sky, which are then further subdivided into the twelve divisions of the sky known as the astrological houses.

The houses represent twelve situations, circumstances, or persons that all of us contend with at one time or another:

- House 1: self-image, identity; our own behaviors.
- House 2: survival issues, money, banks, purchases.
- House 3: thinking, speaking, reading; driving, excursions; siblings and neighbors.
- House 4: family life, parents, memories, emotions; the home or office.
- House 5: self-expression, creativity, recreation, enjoyment, fun, children.
- House 6: health, employment, self-analysis and self-criticism; aunts and uncles; employees and coworkers.
- House 7: relationships, friendship, and marriage; close friends, spouse, and open adversaries.
- House 8: shared financial resources, sex and emotional intimacy; credit and loans; partner's finances.
- House 9: personal beliefs, education, teachers, travel.
- House 10: professional concerns, career, bosses, authority figures, and the dominant parent.
- House 11: social awareness, participation in politics, professional organizations, and groups in general.
- House 12: solitude, voluntary retreat, introspection, altruistic actions, meditation, dreams, fantasy, prayer.

Each of the twelve houses is associated with one of the twelve signs, with which it shares many themes in common. For example, the meaning of house 1 shares themes correlating to the first sign, Aries. House 5 has much in common with the fifth sign, Leo. House 7 shares themes in common with Libra.

Transits and Progressions

The planets are placed in various houses of our birth charts, and some natal houses may be empty. However, at one time or another each of us experiences the issues pertaining to all twelve houses because after birth the planets continue to travel through the sky. This phenomenon is known as planetary transits. Transits show us what areas of life are demanding our attention at a given time. They offer challenges and opportunities for us to grow and change, and enable us to identify the timing of events with great precision.

The character of transits is determined by the nature of both the transiting planets and the natal planets contacted, as well as the houses involved. Usually when people seek counseling or psychotherapy they are undergoing powerful transits of the outer planets, Uranus, Neptune, and Pluto, which often correspond to major transformations of perspective and behavior. Pluto transits may correspond to traumatic episodes, emergence of repressed feelings or latent capacities, or experiences of renewal and rebirth. During Neptune transits we often experience dissolution of structures and loss of focus, or an awakening of our imagination. Uranus transits give an urge for freedom, new directions, and rapid change. Saturn transits challenge us to develop greater maturity, to accept responsibility, and to achieve our goals through sustained, focused effort. Jupiter transits are periods for planning, expansion, and opportunity; these are times when we perceive new horizons and possibilities. Mars transits are periods for action, initiative, and exertion of energy. Transits of Venus harmonize our lives, making events and relationships flow easily, while Mercury's transits show the changing focus of our attention and our conscious thought processes. The Moon's transits indicate the constantly changing focus of our moods and circumstances.

Another technique astrologers use for understanding the timing of events is to "progress" the birth chart. Here we examine how the birth pattern changes and unfolds over time. While there are numerous methods of progressing the horoscope, the two main methods used are known as *secondary progressions* and *solar arc directions.* In secondary progressions, we examine the changing positions of the planets in the days immediately after a person's birth. Each day after birth is viewed as symbolically equivalent to one year of personal growth. Thus, the positions of the planets on the thirtieth day after birth is considered an indicator of the person's condition in the thirtieth year of life. In secondaries, each planet moves at its own intrinsic rate of motion. Since the transiting Moon moves between 11–15° per *day,* the progressed Moon moves 11–15° per *year;* in contrast, the progressed Sun moves between 57' and 61' (minutes) of arc (approximately 1°) per year — corresponding to the transiting Sun's daily motion. The slower, outer planets move only a few minutes of arc per year by secondary progression. In contrast, solar arc directions move all the natal planets forward at a uniform rate, approximately a degree per year — determined by calculating the distance between the natal Sun and its secondary progressed position. If the Sun has progressed 20° 10' from its natal position, then all the planets are directed forward by that arc. Major progressed or solar arc aspects are reliable way of making projections about the course of life and challenges and opportunities in the past, present, and future.[9]

Transits and progressions are two of the methods that are the basis for the unique predictive power of astrology. This book is less focused on teaching the mechanics of these techniques, for we are more concerned here with making the bridge between planetary symbols and the counseling process. Nevertheless, I would like to briefly demonstrate how transits and progressions can be utilized to quickly identify the timing of crucial events with great therapeutic effectiveness.

For example, the birth chart often contains clear indicators of family crises in the person's early life that may have lasting impact on the individual. A woman named Leslie with Neptune in her 4th house (family) at 10° Scorpio 57, squaring Saturn, came from an extended family with rampant alcoholism (Neptune) and both parents physically debilitated. Noting that her IC was 6° Scorpio 54, four degrees away from natal Neptune, I inferred that in all likelihood the sorrows (Neptune) of her family were particularly severe at age four, when the solar arc IC would have reached the conjunction with Neptune. Leslie was amazed that I could pinpoint so accurately the time in her life when her mother was hospitalized for an extended period, financial woes were pronounced, and the family situation became extremely unstable and chaotic (Neptune). But beyond her amazement at astrology's precision, this observation opened up a fruitful

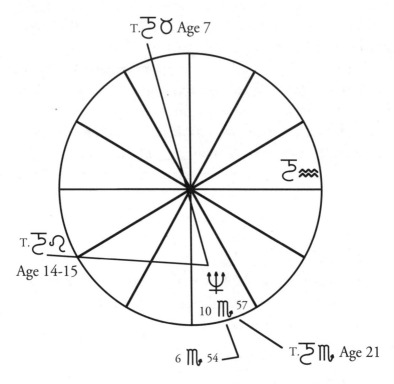

Solar Arc IC conjunct Neptune
Age 4

Leslie

discussion of Leslie's emotional experience at this early stage of her life. I was also able to examine further contacts to this same sensitive planet in her birth chart that might be relevant to her life development. Indeed, many of the central events of her early life had revolved around the symbolism of Neptune.

I went on to note that transiting Saturn was opposite natal Neptune at age seven and inquired about further problematic developments in her family life at this time. Leslie reported that she had submerged her own identity in caring for others in her family, most notably her disabled mother. When Saturn squared Neptune from Leo at age fourteen, her father was stricken with a life threatening illness, her mother became fanatically religious, and Leslie got involved in drug use. Also in keeping with the symbolism of Neptune, she now began to develop a pattern of numbing and dissociating from her feelings as a way of shutting out her internal responses to situations she could not control. This became an important issue in her therapy. At age twenty-one, while Saturn was conjunct Neptune, Leslie had difficulties with housing, living in dilapidated apartments (Neptune in 4th), and feeling lost and estranged from her family. Identifying these crucial periods from the past provided rich material for exploration in counseling.[10]

Examining Leslie's birth chart enabled us to look forward as well. Noting that transiting Jupiter was about to pass through her 4th house and to come into conjunction with natal Neptune, we discussed her desire for a calm, safe, expansive home, for unconditional emotional acceptance, and for healing and reconciliation with her family. All of this came to pass during the year of this transit. She found a beautiful, quiet, meditative (Neptune) home in the woods, began to speak with her parents after many years of little contact, and began to feel more emotionally centered and content. This transit to her Neptune corresponded to a time when Leslie began to experience peace in nature and in her personal environment (4th house), and when her drug use ceased completely.

This example demonstrates how astrological observations help us anticipate the client's central concerns and guide our intuition about the person so that we can access the appropriate tools from our repertoire as counselors. The remarkably accurate techniques of transits and progressions illuminate the person's unfolding along the dimension of time. They allow us to perceive the sequence of events and experiences that have become the central themes, memories, and turning points in the individual's life. Numerous examples throughout this book will illustrate how knowledge of these methods can be utilized to focus the counseling process, to inform our interventions, and to catalyze positive change.

The basic symbols discussed in this chapter — the ten major planets, their sign and house placements, their aspects to one another, and their transiting and progressed positions — are the foundation of astrology. Understanding this planetary language gives counselors and therapists access to profound insights about their clients. In the next chapter we will begin to correlate astrological symbolism with the issues commonly addressed in the course of psychotherapy.

CHAPTER THREE

The Signs and Houses as Symbols of Therapeutic Issues

The practice of therapeutic astrology begins when we first examine a client's birth chart and translate its symbolism into the language of the therapeutic process. Each birth map has particular areas of emphasis that help us understand the person and the likely focus of counseling. We note the sign and house placement of the natal Sun, Moon, Saturn, and ruler of the Ascendant; planets in the same sign or house of the birth chart, or those involved in strong aspects. We also pay special attention to planets near the four major angles of the chart.[11] Each of these planets will have great importance in the person's life. Most importantly, we closely examine the house and sign placement of each planet.

One of the effective ways to apply astrology to the counseling process is to view the twelve signs and houses as symbols of central psychological needs and therapeutic issues, as well as specific approaches to treatment that are likely to be pertinent in our work with a particular client. This chapter summarizes some of the treatment concerns associated with the signs and houses and illustrates these with brief case examples. By examining each planetary position carefully, the astrotherapist quickly develops a sense of the challenges that bring the client to counseling. It is important to note that in our work with each person, many of the issues that I outline here may become therapeutic concerns if we take into account planetary aspects, transits, and progressions.

Aries / 1st House

Aries signifies our need for spontaneous action, unbridled by the need to think first or consider other people. A significant emphasis on planets in Aries or the 1st house may indicate that the person needs to learn to act more instinctively and assertively, or to express desires and impulses in appropriate ways. For example, Mark, a forty-five-year-old man with Sun in Aries in the 5th house opposite Neptune, finds it difficult to control his tendency to drink, gamble, and party wildly despite the damage this does to his career and personal relationships. Mark needs to learn impulse control and to find ways of having fun and celebrating (Sun in 5th house, the house of play and recreation) without excessive inebriation (Neptune).

Brad, a man with Sun in Aries square Mars, had many difficulties stemming from his fierce competitiveness, combativeness, and selfishness — all qualities associated with the sign of Aries and its planetary ruler, Mars. He punched holes in walls and battered his wife. Brad's work focused on gaining insight into the sources of his anger and learning to express his abundant energy in more constructive ways.

An example of a person who needed to become more assertive was Hillary, a woman who had Moon in Aries quin- ☽ ⚻ ♆ cunx Neptune in the 1st house. With Neptune in the 1st, she ♈ 1st exhibited a doe-eyed kind of innocence and had largely suppressed the side of her that loved fun and acting on a whim. Her humble, unassuming nature obscured the true depths of her emotional needs (Moon) and personal desires (Aries). A dream emerged that crystallized her predicament and jarred loose important childhood memories (Moon). In the dream, Hillary was three years old and was screaming for her mother, who was selfish and completely unresponsive to her child. As her mother ignored her cries, Hillary felt both profoundly guilty and completely invisible. This dream brought her the realization that she had spent her whole life in this same state of guilt and invisibility, assuming that she had no right to ask for anything and that no one would ever be attentive to her wishes. She had learned to silence herself, not making a peep about her needs, and never directly pursuing her own desires in life. Hillary's therapy began with a process of learning that she had a right to want things, without apology. ☉ ☿ ♂ ♈

A woman with Sun, Mercury, and Mars in Aries in the 8th house reported that she started having affairs six months after her marriage. Since then she had carried on relationships with a large number of sexual partners (Sun conjunct Mars, 8th house emphasis). She felt entitled to do whatever she wanted, whenever the impulse struck her, and she felt no empathy or concern for her husband, who eventually divorced her (the 8th house also governs divorce). Her preoccupation with getting

her way and satisfying her every desire exemplifies the predicament of a person with an emphasis on the sign of Aries, who
often finds it difficult to accommodate the needs of others.
Quite often the issue with Aries is whether we can get what we
want, without hurting someone else to get it.

The 1st house is concerned with self-awareness and
identity formation. Thus, planets placed in the 1st house,
either natally or by transit, will nearly always point to
significant issues concerning clarification of self-image. This
is a crucial area of the chart because it concerns an individual's
capacity to clearly define and express his or her essential
identity, rather than an inauthentic social mask (persona).

Doris, a thirty-one-year-old
woman who came for counseling
in the midst of a turbulent identity crisis, had five planets in
her 1st house — a Venus-Uranus
conjunction in late Cancer and a
Sun-Mars-Jupiter conjunction in
early Leo. Doris was in profound conflict regarding her

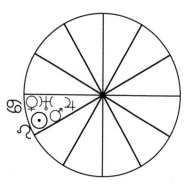

sexual identity. Aptly expressing the unconventionality of her
Venus-Uranus conjunction, she was a politically active, radical
feminist who had been exclusively lesbian throughout her
twenties. With Sun conjunct Mars and Jupiter in the 1st house,
she was extremely concerned with being physically strong,
prided herself on her muscular (Mars) physique, and tended to
be the more dominant, aggressive partner in any relationship.
Doris was confused because her tough, Martian, masculine
traits and behaviors had not completely displaced the more

feminine, Venusian part of her that was concerned about beauty and her attractiveness to men. When I first saw her, she was acutely "heterophobic," that is, afraid of turning into a heterosexual. She gradually began to redefine her sexual identity as bisexual, rather than exclusively lesbian.

Planets in the 1st house represents how we define ourselves and present ourselves to the world. A man named Ted with Mars and Uranus in the 1st house, is an actor and dancer whose exuberant, zany (Uranus) energy has electrified film and TV audiences. He has had hundreds of lovers and feels that sexual (Mars) freedom (Uranus) is central to his identity.

A man named Gordon, with Mercury conjunct Neptune in his 1st house, was a pathological liar who constantly distorted and obscured (Neptune) the truth. As I explored this issue with him, I realized that Gordon had an elaborate set of fantasies about himself that he had never shared with anyone before; and that he lied because he did not know how to actually attain his dreams. His tendency to invent reality hid a fundamental uncertainty about his own identity.

Ahmed had Uranus and Pluto conjunct in the 1st house in Virgo. He grew up in an inner city housing project surrounded by gangs, violence, and crime (Pluto). He developed an aura of self-mastery and contained power (Pluto) that he felt had protected him during a long journey through the underworld of humanity — including a prison term for assault and battery. He emanated a toughness that commanded respect as well as fear, yet he was armored so deeply that nobody could reach him emotionally. Throughout his life he had fought within himself with feelings of persecution and self-hatred (Pluto in 1st), as well as with his desire to incite riots and lead armed uprisings in the streets. He felt that his life's purpose was to become a catalyst of social change and a cultural revolutionary (Uranus). The question was how he could accomplish this goal. Ahmed had Gemini on the Midheaven (career) and natal Sun, Mercury, and Neptune in the third house (writing). He wanted to write films, to express his political ideas and his perceptions of human nature, and to see his stories come to life on screen. This aspiration was fully congruent with his desire to be an agent of social transformation. Ahmed enrolled in school to study film-making.

Taurus / 2nd House

A major emphasis in the horoscope on Taurus or the 2nd house (or major transits here) may indicate important treatment issues regarding feelings of basic competency, the desire for material security, physical comfort and pleasure, and money — including concerns regarding payment for therapy. Pertinent issues might include decisions regarding "right livelihood," the responsible use of resources, and efforts to define and satisfy material needs. Taurus and the 2nd house draw us into deeper embodiment and greater solidity in the physical world. Thus, sensory-awareness methods, somatic therapies, as well as practical, problem-centered counseling could all be appropriate treatment approaches to Taurus and 2nd house concerns. In addition, exploration of a client's money issues are often intertwined with underlying concerns about self-worth that may need attention.

A twenty-five-year-old man named Robert came for counseling in a state of deep anxiety regarding the direction of his life, marital tensions, sexual dysfunction, and financial difficulties. Robert's Sun and Moon were in Taurus in the 3rd house opposing Neptune in Scorpio in the 9th house. In addition, he had Mars in Pisces in the 2nd house. When he started therapy, transiting Saturn was opposite his Sun and Moon and opposite Neptune. He was on welfare and

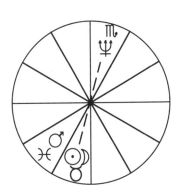

was completely confused (Neptune) about how to pay the mortgage for the house he and his wife had recently purchased with financial assistance from their families. He felt helpless to deal with his problems and spent most of his time stoned on marijuana (Neptune).

Robert's difficulty in finding work gave apt expression to his 2nd house Mars in Pisces, that is, he was confused and passive (Pisces) about money (2nd house) and lacked both the motivation and vitality (Mars) to support himself and his family. Counseling focused on the roots of his wounded self-confidence and his feelings of worthlessness. After some time in therapy, Robert began to earn some money driving a taxi (Sun-Moon in Taurus in the 3rd house, the house of driving), cut down on his drug use, and began to read and write poetry (Neptune opposing Sun-Moon in the 3rd house, which is also the house of reading and writing). Later, after returning to school to complete his degree in biology, Robert found a good paying job as a scientist specializing in water conservation and began to write articles on this topic (Taurus Sun opposite Neptune in house 3). He became more solid, grounded, and practical.

ħ♉
♇ 2nd

A man named Gordon, with Saturn in Taurus and Pluto in the 2nd house, was not comfortable with physical touch or sensual enjoyment of any kind. He was a somewhat dry, ascetic type, who compulsively avoided spending money on anything but the barest necessities. He came from a background of material deprivation and approached life from a stance of scarcity, even though he was now quite well off. Yet deeper exploration revealed a gluttonous, voraciously acquisitive streak that Gordon assiduously resisted and suppressed. Therapy examined his attitudes toward money and physical pleasures and suggested ways to reconstitute his capacity for enjoyment of the physical world.

Gemini / 3rd House
The therapeutic issues of persons with an emphasis on Gemini or the 3rd house often focus on communication problems, self-limiting and destructive beliefs, and learning or speech disorders. Cognitive therapy, "reframing," positive thinking and mental imagery, affirmations, mindfulness, and mental concentration practices might all be useful treatment approaches for people with an emphasis here. Gemini symbolizes language, narrative, the literary arts, and the weaving of tales. Thus, Gemini and the 3rd house concerns can be addressed through writing, through reading and recounting stories, and through techniques like Ira Progoff's intensive journal method. In Robert's case, his 3rd house Sun found expression through gathering information and writing about a topic of keen personal interest, as well as through writing poetry.

A man named Don with Mercury (ruler of Gemini) square Neptune, and Moon in the 3rd house in Pisces (Neptune's sign) wanted to be a writer but felt blocked and inhibited. Part of his difficulty stemmed from the fact that he was trying to write highly structured, academically oriented work, when he was more interested in fiction-writing, poetry, and other imaginative (Neptune) kinds of literature. He became a science fiction writer and eventually had two novels published.

Ann was a quiet, shy woman who found it difficult to speak up in social situations. Her Sun was placed in Cancer in the 3rd house squaring Neptune. She was alexythymic, meaning that she was unable to verbalize her feelings (Sun in 3rd house of communication, in Cancer, the sign of emotions). I encouraged her to recount the most sig- 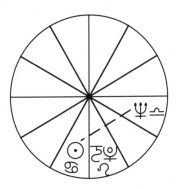 nificant events of her life story through journal writing. She awakened her voice and linked her personal feelings and memories (Cancer) to universal themes by reading books on mythology and by practicing dreamwork (Sun square Neptune).

Gemini and the 3rd house are concerned with communication. A woman named Amy with Mercury conjunct Venus in Gemini in the 1st house had a strong need for lively conversation with a partner. She came for couples counseling with her boyfriend Darrel, who had natal Mars and Saturn in the 3rd house. Amy complained that Darrel was taciturn and uncommunicative, never listened to her, and became angry and impatient with Amy's "small talk." Initially I focused on improving Darrel's communication skills (eye contact, listening, responding), as well as helping Amy understand his different communication needs. Deeper work revealed that Darrel had come from a family in which he was expected to remain quiet and rarely allowed to speak up.

Since the 3rd house governs brothers and sisters, an emphasis here can indicate significant issues related to siblings, as well as neighbors and roommates. Allison, a woman with Mercury-Mars in her 3rd house in Scorpio, experienced protracted conflict (Mars) with her brother over their joint management of family assets (Scorpio). Her brother often yelled profanities at her and generally treated her with contempt and cruelty. Her natal Sun was in Libra and she was essentially a kind, accommodating person who wanted to get along with others. She felt completely tongue-tied, intimidated, and unable to cope with her brother. I encouraged Allison to engage this conflict directly, standing up for herself and speaking forcefully (Mercury-Mars in 3rd) in her own behalf, rather than backing down to her brother's demands.

A man with a Venus-Neptune conjunction in his 3rd house idealized his brother, whom he perceived as superior to him in every way. A woman named Jenny, with Moon conjunct Pluto in her 3rd house, felt terrorized by her roommate, whose hostile, controlling behaviors evoked memories of Jenny's mother (Moon).

Gemini represents the internal stream of thought and "self-talk," the flow of ideas, concepts, and opinions that we hold about life and about ourselves. A man named Ken had Sun in Libra squaring Saturn in the 3rd house. He was a talented and personable artist whom everybody liked. Yet he was full of negative thoughts about himself and his work. Deeper exploration revealed that he had a very conservative, professionally successful brother (Saturn in Capricorn in 3rd house) who had made many disparaging comments about Ken's artistic career and his poor financial prospects. I introduced Ken to very basic cognitive therapy principles, such as observing negative, self-attacking thoughts, identifying the situations that triggered them, and correcting these thoughts to be more self-affirming. Changing his thinking freed Ken from his fear of failure and allowed him to become more serious about pursuing his chosen profession.

Cancer / 4th House

Cancer and the 4th house refer to some of the central domains of psychotherapy: feelings, personal memories, and the family of origin. A significant emphasis here may show the need to clarify and work through issues related to early childhood, relationships with parents, the presence or absence of emotional sustenance in the family, or family pathology and the intergenerational transmission of dysfunctional behaviors. Of course, early family dynamics greatly affect a person's ability to feel emotionally contented in home and family life as an adult. A 4th house emphasis natally or by transit may suggest a need to focus on the client's dependency needs, feelings of emotional security, and capacity for self-soothing, self-care, as well as nurturing of others. This is the realm of family therapy and psychoanalytically oriented depth psychotherapy, which focus upon healing through exploration of family dynamics and emotional memories.

A woman named Phyllis had natal Saturn in Cancer on the Midheaven squaring Moon (ruler of Cancer) and Neptune in her 1st house. She came to therapy to address her feelings of weakness, insecurity, and low self-esteem. These issues were traced back to problems in her family of origin (Saturn in Cancer), specifically an enmeshed, emotionally fused relationship with her alcoholic mother (Moon conjunct Neptune, which rules weak boundaries).

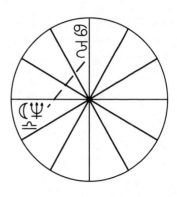

Mother had always acted like a helpless, self-pitying martyr (Neptune) and Phyllis had played the role of her placator, caretaker, and "enabler." She was a highly serious, parentified child who suppressed her emotions (Moon square Saturn in Cancer) and concentrated on the responsibilities of taking care of everyone else in the family. Phyllis also had many traumatic interactions with her father, a tyrannical man who eroded (Neptune) her self-confidence (Saturn) by telling her that she was stupid and incompetent. Counseling addressed these issues in depth, and helped Phyllis gain new confidence. She began to trust her feelings and intuitions and to learn that she could be open, emotionally aware, and sensitive to others (Moon-Neptune) without being taken advantage of, without being a doormat for others to walk upon.

A thirty-three-year-old Jewish woman named Sara had Venus, Saturn, and Sun in Scorpio and in her 4th house, closely square the Moon in Aquarius in the 7th house (relationships). Our initial work focused on her parents' vehement disapproval of her previous relationship of five years duration to a man of another race (Aquarian Moon in the 7th house squaring her 4th house planets). We examined Sara's difficult relationship with her parents and her feelings of anger and resentment (Scorpio) toward them. An important memory of sexually abuse by one of her brothers surfaced as transiting Pluto — planet of emergence of repressed material — formed a conjunction to natal Saturn. (Natal Mars, co-

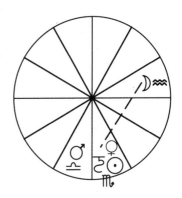

ruler of Scorpio, was placed in her 3rd house, which rules brothers.) Her story had a happy ending: As natal Venus and Saturn moved by solar arc direction from the square of natal Moon to a sextile, she was married in a traditional Jewish wedding ceremony with her proud parents in attendance. However, in accordance with the progressive, unconventional attitude in the choice of relational partners signified by her Aquarius Moon in the 7th house, Sara married a Catholic.

A woman named Ellen had her first child when transiting Saturn and Uranus were conjunct her natal Moon in the 1st house. Ellen said that becoming a mother (Moon) and starting a family was the most significant decision of her life. Now she was able to fully express her

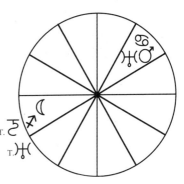

nurturing, emotionally sensitive qualities. Ellen also had a conjunction of natal Mars and Uranus in Cancer, the sign of home, family, and property. When transiting Uranus opposed natal Mars-Uranus, her house burned to the ground in a large urban fire (Mars), reducing to ashes years of love and effort that she had expended to create a beautiful home. This resulted in a period of major emotional upheaval (Cancer), family reorganization, and eventually a move to a more rural location where she and her husband built a new home. Here Ellen began to rediscover the beauty of the land and the joys of domestic activities like cooking and gardening. Astrologically informed counseling helped her understand the meaning of these unexpected changes and encouraged her to make the transition into this new lifestyle.

Ann (mentioned above) had Saturn and Pluto conjunct in her 4th house in Leo. Her father was a physically violent, abusive (Pluto) alcoholic (Sun square Neptune). She came to therapy quite depressed (Saturn-Pluto) after separating from her husband. At the time, transiting Saturn was in Aquarius, opposing natal Saturn-Pluto. Her marriage had repeated many of the abusive dynamics of her parents' marriage (Pluto, ruler of Scorpio on 7th house cusp, in the 4th house.) Pluto in her 4th house suggested that Ann's quiet demeanor masked many suppressed feelings — fury, shock, deep rivers of emotion. In therapy, much repressed material emerged (Pluto) as she retrieved memories of traumatic episodes from both her family of origin and her own marriage. Her road to emotional healing was a long one, yet she faced her fears and her pain and grew stronger.

Leo / 5th House

Leo and the 5th house represent our need to feel and express joy, and our capacity for enthusiasm, playfulness, and exuberance. Children, self-expression, and creativity are central concerns of this sign and house. Zipporah Dobyns associates Leo and the 5th house with the need to love and be loved, to feel our creative power, and to be a shining star that the world will admire.[12] Persons with strong emphasis here may have commanding personalities with great poise and presence. In some cases, they may also need to address psychological issues of narcissism, such as feelings of specialness, superiority, or entitlement. Therapy addressing Leo or 5th house issues might focus on finding appropriate means of self-expression, whether this is through athletics, musical, artistic, or theatrical performance, dance, or other fun, recreational activities. Expressive therapies such as psychodrama, art therapy, or dance therapy, or work to overcome creative blocks may be indicated when these areas are emphasized natally. Individuals whose charts highlight Leo or the 5th house often need encouragement to let the full radiance and grandeur of the self shine forth without excessive and unhealthy grandiosity.

Jane, a young woman with the Sun in Leo in the 1st house opposite Saturn, was a talented actress, but described herself as preoccupied with her beauty and efforts to impress others. Jane's Therapy focused on her efforts to freely express her creativity and her sunny, flamboyant, dynamic personality without being overly vain, histrionic, and self-absorbed. She also worked to overcome her deep-seated fear of expressing her love and putting her heart fully into her work and relationships (Leo Sun opposite Saturn in 7th).

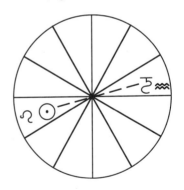

A man with Moon in Scorpio in his 5th house was a stand-up comedian who loved to vent his anger by insulting his audience and performing outrageous (often offensive) jokes with sexual themes (Scorpio). He needed constant admiration from others, and became enraged if he felt in any way slighted or unappreciated, a common manifestation of what psychologists call a narcissistic personality structure.

A twenty-nine-year-old man named Ed had Saturn in the 5th house. During his Saturn Return, he came for counseling complaining of depression and anxiety triggered by the birth of his first child. We discussed the fact that he was experiencing an age-appropriate transition (the Saturn Return) due to the new responsibilities of becoming a father. Soon we uncovered memories of being restricted from playing as a child that seemed to be at the root of Ed's discomfort about having his own children. Ed feared that he would not enjoy playing with his child, that his child would reject him, and that having a child would prevent him from enjoying his own life. As this material was integrated, he became more comfortable with assuming his new parental role.

Sally, age thirty-five, sought counseling about an important decision. She and her husband wanted to have children, but she was not sure her career would leave her adequate time to devote to parenting. Her chart revealed Mercury, Venus, and Neptune in Scorpio in the 5th house, suggesting that children might be a most welcome and satisfying addition to her life. Over the next several years, while transiting Saturn squared these planets from Aquarius, she and her husband had two children. She loves them deeply and feels that they are the source of her deepest fulfillment.

Traditionally the 5th house governed gambling and risk taking. Glen had <u>Saturn in Taurus</u> in the 5th house. He had a compulsive gambling problem and lost large amounts of money betting on horse races and football games (5th house: sports and entertainment). When transiting Pluto squared natal Saturn he began to face up to the fact that he had <u>financial responsibilities</u> to his children (Saturn in Taurus in the 5th house) and that his behavior was endangering their futures. This realization helped him stop gambling.

Joanna worked in a clerical position that she felt was killing <u>her creative spirit</u>. Natal Sun, Venus, and Mars were conjunct in Sagittarius in the 5th house and natal Jupiter and Saturn were in her 6th house. Her real passion was music (Venus); she was a talented musician with a degree in ethnomusicology that she now viewed as completely impractical. In fact, she often berated herself for her naiveté in choosing such a college major. During her Saturn Return she accepted a full-time job and was earning a good salary, yet she <u>felt that an essential part of herself had died</u>. She was starting to feel <u>resigned</u> to staying at this job forever, for at least it provided her with <u>some security</u>.

It was obvious that Joanna was not expressing her greatest talents; and her lack of alignment with her essential identity was manifesting as a <u>nagging sense of sadness and apathy</u>, <u>health problems (Saturn in 6th)</u>, and a loss of interest in people and relationships. Then, when transiting Saturn started to square her natal Sun, Venus, and Mars from Pisces, she began to take some <u>lessons from a noted musician</u>. He invited her to <u>join his band</u> and go on tour with him. <u>In the blink of an eye</u> her life changed. She took a risk (5th house) that she never regretted or doubted, seizing this opportunity to perform and to express her true nature. In the bargain, she also got to travel throughout Europe — which, with her three planets in Sagittarius, was very exciting for her. The final part of the story is even sweeter: In keeping with the romantic symbolism of the Saturn transit to natal Venus and Mars, she and the other musician were married upon returning from their travels.

Virgo / 6th House

Virgo represents our desire for refinement, precision, and perfection, as well as the ability to recognize our mistakes and shortcomings and to correct them. A focus on Virgo or the 6th house may suggest anxiety, nervous tension, obsessive tendencies, a strong "inner critic" or tendency to criticize others, or the need to develop greater discrimination. Virgo and 6th house concerns in therapy may include helping the client to reflect inwardly, scrutinize the self closely, and implement specific means of self-improvement and purification. In some cases, this may indicate a need to undertake dietary changes, an exercise routine, or a spiritual discipline. Virgo or 6th house emphasis may suggest a need to focus on health issues in general and the way in which illness may be understood as an opportunity for transformation. Planets here may also indicate important concerns regarding employment, our daily work duties, or the need for vocational training.

A man named Jeff, with a conjunction of Sun, Saturn, Mercury, and Moon in Virgo in the 7th house, was the son of a family most of whose relatives had been killed in the Holocaust. He was plagued by the classic symptoms of "survivor guilt": He was deeply depressed (Sun-Saturn aspect) and suffered from acute anxiety, phobias, numerous chronic physical complaints (Virgo) verging on hypochondria, and dysphoria (an inability to find any satisfaction or pleasure in everyday living). Jeff was also highly perfectionistic and demanding in his personal relationships.

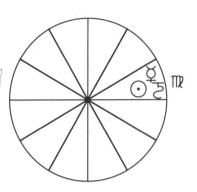

Therapy focused on anxiety reduction methods as well as analysis of his relationship with his father (Saturn), who had constantly criticized Jeff, contributing both to his self-critical nature and his inability to tolerate the imperfections of others.

Clark had a Sun-Pluto conjunction in his 6th house in Leo. He often had unpleasant power struggles (Pluto) with his boss and co-workers and had to perform many boring, demeaning tasks at his job (6th house) that wounded his pride (Leo) and frustrated his desire for

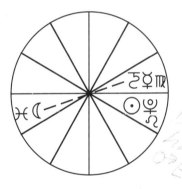

self-expression. Counseling addressed the need to transform his attitude toward work, to learn to have fun on the job, and to find ways to express his creativity through his work and to put his own mark on all of his labors.

Judith had Jupiter in Virgo conjunct her Ascendant. She was a highly conscientious person, a hard worker (Virgo), employed as an international policy analyst (Jupiter: international relations; Virgo: analysis). She had suffered from severe anorexia in her youth, which had significantly damaged her health. She was still obsessively careful and picky about food. I referred her to a clinician specializing in the treatment of eating disorders.

Libra / 7th House

With a Libra or 7th house emphasis, therapy might focus on the client's experience of friendship and marriage, repeating behavioral patterns in relationships, and the way the person loves and seeks completion through others. Planets in the 7th house can also reveal facets of the personality that may be lived through other people. For example, people with Mars in the 7th house often experience their partners as attacking or aggressive. The person may disown these qualities, projecting them onto others, and failing to see how they provoke angry reactions through their own behaviors.

The 7th house represents the individual's subjective experience of being with other people, as well as the kinds of partners he or she tends to attract. A person with Venus in the 7th might attract friendly or attractive friends and partners who are kind and pleasant, and relationships may be fairly harmonious; he or she may be quite eager to please others. With Mars in the 7th house, the individual might attract a sexy, passionate, physically active, or an irritating, argumentative partner or relationship. With this placement, we may tend to put power in the hands of others or act aggressively to try to maintain a dominant position; alternatively, we may engage in healthy competition or actively take steps to help others.[13] With Neptune in the 7th, our partners may be idealistic, imaginative, spiritually oriented visionaries, or spaced out, unfocused, dependent, or deceptive individuals.

With Saturn in the 7th, a person may be attracted to partners who are solid, dependable, conservative, and who may be older or more established in the world. Jane (see Leo section) had natal Saturn in her 7th house opposite her Leo Sun. She was discouraged and sad because she felt disappointed with her marriage. Her husband seemed boring, restrictive, and overly serious to her. In therapy, she came to the realization that she had been searching for a father figure (Saturn) to support her so that she could pursue her career as an actress (Leo Sun). Now that she had found someone who was capable of taking care of her in this manner, she perceived him as rigid and uptight, like her own father. Jane developed a stronger sense of responsibility for her own life and greater appreciation for the reliable, hardworking man she loved and to whom, she realized, she was deeply committed (Saturn in 7th).

Clark (see above) sought counseling after his marriage of seven years broke up. He reported very poor communication with his wife (Mercury-Saturn in 7th house) and that his wife criticized him constantly (Virgo planets). In response to her criticism he developed a pattern of depressed withdrawal (Moon in Pisces opposite Saturn, the planet of depression and sadness). Exploration of his feelings about this marriage revealed a prior history of abandonment, neglect, and criticism. His mother died when he was four years old, leaving him in a state of constant emotional hunger, overwhelmed by feelings of inner emptiness, and loneliness (Moon in Pisces). His father favored his older brother and was stern and strongly disapproving toward Clark (Saturn in Virgo). We

✱ brilliant!

♄ ♍ 7th
☽ ♂ ✱

explored how his early family history directly related to his marital experience, which had been dominated by the fear that his deepest emotional needs and longing to be nurtured would never be seen, acknowledged, or satisfied by his spouse.

Vernon, age 50, had natal Mars, Saturn, and Uranus, in the 7th house in Gemini. He came to therapy to explore marital difficulties that he felt were caused by his wife's insistence on exploring kinky sex (Mars-Uranus) with multiple lovers. In the 7th house our ability to tol-

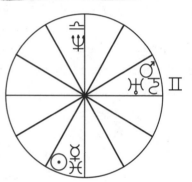

erate closeness with another person is tested. Vernon had significant conflict between his desire for reliable closeness (Saturn in 7th) and his desire for total freedom (Uranus). He had drawn a partner who acted out the conflict for him and whom he could blame for all the problems in their marriage. Vernon began to recognize that his wife's behaviors were a direct reflection of his own ambivalence about closeness.

♄7th
vs
♂ ♅
7th

The 7th house also governs the nature of the therapeutic alliance, which generally parallels the person's broader experience of relationship with others in general. Thus, planets in the 7th house may indicate transference phenomena that need to be addressed in counseling. By examining the client's perception of the therapist in the light of planets placed here, the counselor can gain insight into the client's way of perceiving and experiencing the presence of others — as safe or threatening, helpful or demanding, benign or cruel, passive or pushy, stuffy or unpredictable. As planets in the 7th house suggest important relational themes that tend to repeat, they can also provide important clues to the nature of the countertransference that may be evoked in the therapist.

A man named Todd with Mars in his 7th house made me intensely <u>uncomfortable</u> during all of our sessions. He often became angry with me, and I, in turn, often became irritated and angry with him. Knowledge of his birth chart symbolism helped me keep my own countertransference feelings in perspective and to explore with Todd the ways in which close relationships with other people tended to evoke a great deal of anger. In contrast, a woman named Victoria, with Neptune in her 7th house, had what Heinz Kohut calls an "idealizing transference," viewing me as perfect in every way.[14] In her therapy Victoria had to work through her disappointment and upset when, inevitably, I failed to live up to her image of perfection. This was a direct reenactment of the feelings she had experienced in many of her personal relationships. Gradually she learned to see me (and others) more realistically.

A thirty-one-year-old woman named Debbie came for counseling while transiting Saturn was conjunct her natal Sun in Scorpio in the 7th house. She had been fighting violently with her boyfriend for several months. After several sessions Debbie began to behave in a seductive manner, wearing revealing clothing, looking at me with an inviting gaze, and openly discussing her erotic fantasies about me. By examining this behavior in the light of her birth chart symbolism, we discovered her <u>tendency to use sexuality</u> as a <u>substitute</u> for genuine <u>intimacy</u>, a means of establishing closeness when she felt <u>insecure</u>, of attempting to <u>gain control over others</u>, and of energizing a basically depleted sense of self. Examination of the transference was a major turning point in Debbie's therapy.

With emphasis on planets placed in Libra, the individual may have a strong urge to create beauty or pursue interests in the arts. A social worker with Sun conjunct Venus in Libra in her 10th house began to cry during a session when I suggested that she might have really wanted to become a musician. We discussed ways she could incorporate her love of music through training in music therapy, which she later reported was very effective with her patients.

Scorpio / 8th House

Scorpio is the phase of the zodiac that concerns transformation and the generation of power through the intensities of human interaction. Emphasis on this sign or the 8th house often indicates significant issues regarding sexuality, business relationships, joint financial resources, power, and aggression. For example, a man named Jack with Mars in Scorpio and in the 8th house came to therapy because of his violent temper. He was also preoccupied with sexual fantasies involving the power dynamics of domination and submission.

In therapy, Scorpio or 8th house issues may focus upon the way in which the client directs hostility toward the therapist, sexualizes the relationship (like Debbie), or perceives the therapist as hostile, seductive, or intrusive. In some instances, emphasis here may suggest the need to address paranoia, suicidality, post-traumatic stress disorder, or memories of physical trauma or sexual abuse. This region can also be associated with tendencies toward devaluation of others, explosions of rage, and ruptures in the empathic connection between therapist and client. Sex therapy, crisis counseling, Reichian therapy, or other cathartic methods such as primal scream, rebirthing, or holotropic breathwork may be appropriate here in some cases. Other therapeutic concerns often seen when there is an emphasis here in the chart are issues stemming from interpersonal crisis, divorce, debt, death of friend, relative, or spouse, or a personal brush with death.

Working through the issues connected with Scorpio and the 8th house provides some of the most intense moments in the therapeutic journey. Nevertheless, the death and rebirth often experienced in addressing these issues may bring about deep personal renewal. It is only when therapy reaches these levels that the client's character structure begins to shift and therapy becomes a true initiation into a new state of being.

Richard, age fifty, with Sun in Scorpio conjunct his Ascendant, frequently expressed rage toward the many people whom he felt were persecuting, humiliating, disappointing, and plotting against him. He was filled with spite, resentment, vengeful feelings, hostility, and paranoia. We managed to avoid serious empathic ruptures until one day, with transiting Saturn exactly conjunct his natal Sun, he began to devalue me, listing my many perceived inadequacies and saying that I had failed him like everyone else in his life. A storm of foul language followed. Despite my efforts to reestablish contact with Richard, I was unable to contain his angry outburst and he stormed out of the session, never to return.

Gina had Sun, Mercury, Venus, and Jupiter in Pisces in the 8th house opposed by Saturn in the 2nd. Gina built a successful business with her husband. But when transiting Saturn and Uranus squared these natal planets from Sagittarius, Gina's

husband unexpectedly stole all
of their money and ran off to
Las Vegas with a girlfriend. She
was devastated over their divorce, the loss of her business,
and the fact that she was left to
raise five children alone (Pisces:
abandonment issues). Her husband later declared bankruptcy

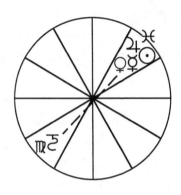

and refused to pay child support. She had much work to do to
contend with their joint debts (8th house emphasis) and her
disillusionment after their breakup. Pisces rules illusions: Gina
was stripped of her illusions about her husband fairly quickly,
and now saw that she had been in denial (Pisces), failing to see
the obvious warning signs of his infidelity. She also
recognized the need to become more practical about earning
her own income and more organized in handling her finances
(Saturn in 2nd house).

Elaine, with Sun-Mercury-Venus-Neptune in Scorpio in
the 8th house, was the daughter of a very puritanical minister.
While Pluto transited over her Scorpio planets, she became
quite sexually active and came to grips with the strong
internalized religious judgments she had about expressing the
lusty, passionate dimension of her personality. Unfortunately,
during this period Elaine also contracted a sexually trans-
mitted disease, and ultimately developed cancer of the
cervix. Her therapeutic process required a brave confrontation
with the possibility that she might die. She survived, shaken to
her core, but transformed by her confrontation with the
elemental forces of sex and death.

When transiting Saturn passed through the 8th house of a man named Douglas, he faced the impending death of his father, the first time he had ever confronted mortality. Reading books on death and dying by writers like Stephen Levine and Elisabeth Kubler-Ross enabled Douglas to understand his emotional reactions, especially his grief and his fear. This inner work, in turn, enabled him to help his father die peacefully, surrounded by love and acceptance.

Nicki had Sun in Scorpio squaring Mars, Pluto (co-rulers of Scorpio), and Saturn in Leo. At the age of seven, while transiting Saturn was conjunct her natal Sun and square Mars, Saturn, and Pluto, her father (Saturn) beat her severely after she was caught engaging in sex-

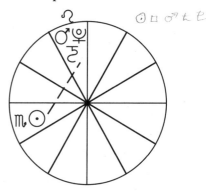

ual play at school. Nicki had never fully recovered from this incident, suffering from post-traumatic stress disorder and many difficulties with sex and intimacy. She was terrified of men, whom she felt were constantly making unwanted and intrusive sexual advances toward her. When she did become intimate with a man, intense anger frequently emerged, and she often perceived her partners as cruel and vindictive (Mars-Pluto square Sun). Counseling addressed her childhood physical trauma, her complex sexual feelings and defenses, and her tendency to externalize anger onto the men in her life. I also encouraged her to take a women's self defense class to learn strategies she could utilize in situations of real threat. A major emotional catharsis led to new feelings of inner power.

Sagittarius / 9th House

Sagittarius is associated with the search for truth and moral values. With planets in Sagittarius or the 9th house, educational concerns and reevaluation of our beliefs are often pertinent themes. Therapeutic concerns focused on this sign or the 9th house may revolve around a loss of meaning and the desire to discover a coherent and clearly defined system of ethical, spiritual, or religious belief. Accordingly, therapy may focus on helping clients develop a personal philosophy that imbues life with hope and meaning. Existential therapy, logotherapy, vision quests, pilgrimages, and the examination of profound philosophical and moral questions may be appropriate. For example, a young woman named Brigit with Sun, Venus, and Mars in Sagittarius was working in the field of publishing (ruled by Sagittarius) but felt stifled and longed for adventure. Understanding her birthmap affirmed Brigit's desire for travel. She left her job to travel for several years in Asia, where she studied Yoga and Buddhist meditation with several great teachers and went on pilgrimages to many sacred religious sites.

A man with Sun and Mercury in Capricorn in the 9th house opposite Jupiter in Cancer and square Neptune in Libra became a renowned spiritual teacher who traveled around the world giving classes and workshops.

Allison had Mars, Saturn, and Uranus in her 9th house in Gemini. She was a highly skilled special education teacher, once described as a "master educator." With her three planets in Gemini (language, communication), Allison specialized in working with children with learning disabilities, especially problems with language and speech. She sought counseling regarding a career change. However, after attempting several other careers she always returned to this work, which seemed to closely match the symbolism of her natal chart. She began to be more content with her career in education and decided that her desire for new learning and mental stimulation (Gemini planets) could be satisfied by training to become a school administrator.

Frank, with Sun conjunct Neptune in Libra in the 9th house, had been in graduate school for many years, unable to complete his dissertation in astrophysics. His professors berated him for being hopelessly impractical, a dreamer and romantic whose interests in cosmology would never draw any solid research funding or give him any chance of professional advancement. His chart indicated that he had the potential to be an intellectual visionary of sorts, yet he reported that his faculty advisor was trying to direct his studies toward highly detailed technical analysis, which seemed unsuitable for his Sun-Neptune nature. He switched advisors, completed his dissertation, and went on to write an award winning book about cosmology.

A woman named Celeste, who had always been rather closed minded toward religion, metaphysics, and the occult, went on an unexpected journey to Sedona, Arizona when transiting Uranus and Neptune passed into her 9th house. She was exposed to a completely different world view — including many "new age" ideas that answered many of her deepest questions about life's meaning. Her twin sister, Lisa, had the same transit at the same time; she became a born-again, fundamentalist Christian. Both Lisa and Celeste experienced a radical shift in their beliefs.

in Cap.
Jupiter (close to 11)
Prog. Sun on cusp of 10 + 11

Capricorn / 10th House

Capricorn is the sign concerned with success, achievement, and the embodiment of one's beliefs and ideals through work and vocation. Therapy addressing Capricorn or 10th house concerns may focus upon career counseling, workaholism, the client's ability to define ambitions and realistically assess personal capabilities, and the need to define vocational goals in relation to existing social institutions.[15] Clients may need encouragement to claim their own authority, to pursue their true ambitions, and to claim for themselves some form of leadership role in the world.

A woman named Nadia with Sun, Mercury, and Venus in the 10th house described herself as a workaholic, driven to achieve success but with no time left for herself. We identified steps she could take to live a more balanced life so that amidst the pressures of her career she could also make time for other interests and pursuits, such as art, music, and relationships (Venus).

Zelda, a woman with Neptune in her 10th house, came to me for career counseling. She hated the competitive atmosphere of most offices, had difficulty staying focused on tasks that she found boring, and longed for a career with a little more glamour. She had done psychic readings professionally for some time but she was looking for something a little steadier. Keying on the symbolism of Neptune, I asked her if she had ever considered becoming a professional photographer. The idea appealed to her greatly. She took some classes, and within three years she was doing this work full time.

Elizabeth, with Mars and Pluto conjunct in Leo in her 10th house, was a successful corporate marketing executive.

Periodically, however, organizational crises and power struggles (Pluto) within her company caused her to become angry and defensive. She also became highly stressed out and broke out in rashes (Mars-Pluto) that covered most of her body. Counseling supported her during a major challenge to her position from the senior managers of her company. She felt they were manipulating her, failing to give her credit for her work, and trying to force her to transfer to a different division or to leave the company altogether. As she identified the source of her angry feelings, she felt able to remain calm as she prepared her response. She weathered the storm effectively, presenting her grievances to the managers with strength, composure, and dramatic flair, maintaining her dignity (Mars in Leo).

A man named Allan, with Sun in Taurus in the 7th house squaring Saturn in Leo in the 10th house, was married and had several children. He had a high paying job that demanded long hours and endless responsibility. He longed for escape, scheming ways he could retire 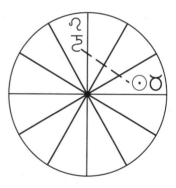 early and live a life of sensual bliss (Taurus Sun) in Hawaii. A major focus of counseling was the need for him to accept that his wife and family depended on his income (Taurus Sun in 7th house) and that for the time being it was necessary for him to fulfill the responsibilities of fatherhood (Saturn in Leo in the 10th). He also recognized the need to be completely practical by taking advantage of the opportunities for long-range financial security his career offered him (Saturn square

Taurus Sun). This knowledge helped Allan affirm his life's path and to feel proud of his accomplishments and his commitment to his children (Saturn in Leo).

Aquarius / 11th House

Nep. Cap
Uranus σ ℞

The sign Aquarius represents our need to be progressive, to rebel against convention, and to explore the cutting edge of invention, science, and discovery. Aquarius and the 11th house are also concerned with an individual's relationship to processes of social change, awareness of current political issues, and capacity to respond to historical circumstances. With a significant emphasis on Aquarius or the 11th house, therapy may focus on establishing a support network, understanding the larger social context of individual problems, and gaining a sense of being a participant in the process of political change and social evolution. Some individuals may need counseling regarding their involvement in cults, new age communities, collectives, social change movements, or political activism. Involvement in groups of various kinds are often indicated for people with an emphasis here — for example, group therapy, men's or women's groups, Twelve Step meetings, professional associations, or attending conferences.

Liza has Venus and Saturn in Aquarius, quincunx Uranus in Virgo. She wears outrageous, colorful clothes, has a unique painting style, and is involved in a politically active group of artists who stage experimental, multi-media events. One of her primary goals is to keep alive the idealism and revolutionary spirit that flourished in the 1960s.

Jill has Saturn and Uranus in the 11th house. She works with corporations and large seminar groups promoting practical strategies and technologies for social change, especially those involving a heightened environmental consciousness. She is particularly interested in solar energy, biodynamic gardening, and innovative solutions to urban housing problems, such as co-housing projects.

A woman named Paula, with natal Saturn and Pluto in Leo in the 11th house opposite the Moon in Aquarius, has been involved in a large and influential spiritual growth movement for over twenty years. In the mid 1980s, while transiting Saturn and Pluto in Scorpio 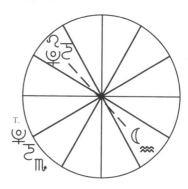 squared natal Saturn-Pluto, she faced the shadows of the movement as she witnessed serious abuses of power (Pluto) among the group's leadership. Eventually she was called upon to assume more responsibility within the group as a teacher and administrator. In counseling, we focused upon how the difficult experiences of strife and power struggles within the organization had taught her essential lessons that could enable her to wield authority (Saturn) appropriately and to become a source of positive leadership.

Brenda had natal Sun in Aquarius in the 5th house, opposite Jupiter in the 11th house. She was an artist whose unique illustrations contained themes of interracial equality and harmony, the struggle for human rights, progressive political activity, and the gathering of individuals into communities. She was an outspoken activist who constantly educated herself (Jupiter) about social issues.

Pisces / 12th House

Pisces and the 12th house represent our need for openness and sense of connection to all and everything. This sign and house are associated with spiritual growth and inner vision, dreams, fantasy life, intuition, and psychic awareness. In other cases, planets in Pisces or the 12th house indicate states of passivity, vulnerability, or lack of focus. These planets may also point to areas where the client feels ineffective, victimized, or powerless. Occasionally, planets placed here are associated with some of the more serious forms of psychopathology, such as delusions, hallucinations, inflation, loss of discriminative faculties, decompensation (falling apart), or even psychosis and institutionalization. More typically, persons with planets in Pisces or the 12th house may need to address alcoholism, addiction, codependency, ACA issues, or feelings of victimization, abandonment, loneliness, or grief.

Pisces and the 12th house represent our desire to turn inward; they signify the healthy process of loosening the tight grip of our rational minds and interiorizing our awareness — which often results in upsurgence of material from the depths of the collective unconscious or experiences of expanded consciousness. Here we may also learn to live a "symbolic life," the ability to view our personal experiences as archetypal and universal, and thus carrying inherent spiritual significance.[16]

Access to archetypal material and transpersonalization of personal identity can be facilitated by hypnosis, guided visualization, dreamwork, active imagination, and other techniques of symbolic amplification. Transpersonal therapies are especially relevant here, including Jungian analysis, shamanic journeys, and past-life regression. Meditation may be an important adjunct of psychotherapy.[17] Individuals with a strong Pisces or 12th house emphasis are likely to be drawn toward some kind of contemplative practice and periods of solitude and retreat. We should support these pursuits unless it is apparent that such interests represent an avoidance of conflictual material — what psychologist John Welwood calls "spiritual bypassing." Pisces and the 12th house are also concerned with transcendence of a limited, ego-centered perspective and the awakening of compassion. With emphasis here the person might focus on ways of expressing the spirit of service and loving-kindness in his or her daily life. This is both the fruit and the goal of spiritual practice.

An example of some of the more difficult clinical manifestations of a chart emphasizing planets in Pisces or the 12th house is a man named Philip, a filmmaker with natal Sun, Mercury, and Saturn in Pisces in the 12th house, opposite Neptune (ruler of Pisces). 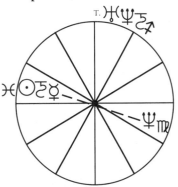 In the mid 1980s, while transiting Saturn, Uranus, and Neptune squared these natal planets from Sagittarius, Philip's career hit the skids and he ended up homeless and drug-addicted. Later he was hospitalized after he developed delusional thoughts and hallucinations. He was fortunate to find a psychiatrist who was interested in Philip's dreams and encouraged him to express his highly developed imagination — a crucial domain of life associated with Pisces, Neptune, and the 12th house. After he had coped with his addiction and his thought disorder subsided, he was released from the hospital and began to write screenplays again.

Vernon (see Libra above), with Sun and Mercury in Pisces and Neptune conjunct his Midheaven, was a chemist for a large pharmaceutical company who had gotten involved in dealing psychedelic drugs. He developed delusions of clairvoyance and enlightenment. For a short time he promoted himself as a spiritual teacher, before recognizing that his actual level of spiritual attainment did not match his fantasy ideal. He was counseled to explore deeper, more genuine mystical states through regular meditation rather than through the use of LSD.

In contrast to the delusions of a person such as Vernon, Tracy — who has Moon, Uranus, and Pluto conjunct in Virgo in the 12th house sextile Neptune in the 2nd — is a psychic with a high degree of accuracy and a large clientele. One of her concerns was how to integrate several powerful and emotionally upsetting past-life memories that emerged spontaneously during meditation.

A woman named Madeline with Moon and Saturn in the 12th house squaring Neptune became debilitated after an accident. She suffered from a degenerative physical condition and spent months convalescing, unable to work. Counseling addressed the feelings of loneliness and helplessness (12th house) brought on by her disability, and assisted her in learning to look inward for meaning rather than solely to outer activities and achievements.

Frieda, with Sun in Pisces quincunx Neptune in the 12th house, has been deeply religious since childhood. She sought counseling during a period when she was seriously considering becoming a nun so she could devote herself to a contemplative

life. However, examination of
her horoscope revealed natal
Mars in the 7th house squaring
Venus, signifying an intense
sexual drive and a desire for
marriage and human compan-
ionship. Thus, a monastic life
did not seem suitable for her.
She decided instead to become

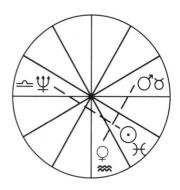

a Jungian analyst. This satisfied her interest in dreams and in
understanding the mysteries of the soul, psyche, and spirit.

Pisces and the 12th house often symbolize the experience
of *liminality* — the condition of transitional uncertainty and
dissolution of prior goals, values, or beliefs that is often
necessary before the reformation of personality can occur. In
Astrology and Spiritual Awakening I described the following
example, which clearly illustrates this, as well as many of the
other issues often faced when 12th house themes are evident. A
twenty-four-year-old man named David sought counseling
during a period of confusion and disorientation. He was
preoccupied with his dreams, and passed most of his time
meditating and reading books about spirituality, psychology,
and mysticism. He was not working or involved in any
relationships. At the time, transiting Neptune was conjunct
natal Saturn, while transiting Saturn was in the 12th house.
Many of David's friends were concerned about his tendency
toward withdrawal and introspection. However, from his birth
chart it was evident that this was a crucial period of inner
work, dissolution of prior identity and interests, and
preparation for the birth of a new self. He began to trust the

appropriateness and necessity of this phase of inner exploration, and allowed himself to immerse himself in it fully, knowing that eventually the period of confusion would end. By the time Saturn transited over his Ascendant, David had become more grounded, willing and able to work, and began a focused process of career planning.

Therapeutic Implications of Rudhyar's Ideas

Psychotherapy is increasingly the setting in which contemporary persons pursue the quest for initiation, metamorphosis, and spiritual rebirth. Contemporary psychotherapy is especially complex because it is often expected to provide three levels of initiation: sociocultural, personal, and transpersonal.[18] That is, people often seek therapy hoping that it will help them to assume a meaningful place in the social order, to discover and express their unique talents and identity, and (in the case of spiritually aware clients) to transcend ordinary ego consciousness in transpersonal states. As we will see in subsequent chapters, astrology can be of great assistance in guiding ourselves and others through these initiatory processes. However, for this purpose we need a multidimensional, spiritually oriented form of astrology.

Dane Rudhyar distinguished four levels of birth chart interpretation: biological (e.g., medical astrology), sociocultural (e.g., vocational astrology), humanistic (e.g., psychologically oriented astrology), and transpersonal.[19] The purpose of astrology at the person-centered or humanistic level is to seek fulfillment as an individual through self-knowledge and self-actualization. In a transpersonal approach to astrology, however, the goal is to facilitate initiation and transition into states of expanded awareness, self-consecration, and spiritually inspired creative activity.[20]

Such a perspective has great relevance for psychotherapists, who are often faced with the task of guiding persons needing guidance at the level of egoic formation and development, yet who also feel an interior calling to a life of higher transformation. Counselors and therapists can utilize astrology to understand the competing needs and developmental strivings of clients struggling to make the transition between "personhood" (sociocultural success and self-actualization) and "seedhood" (self-transcendence and transpersonal creativity). In facilitating such transitions, the counselor or therapist will often be faced with the question of whether the essential priority should be to promote a client's social adjustment and personal fulfillment, or to cooperate with a process of transformation that is often tumultuous and may disrupt egoic stability.

My own view is that the focus of therapeutic work must be determined on an individual basis in accordance with the client's needs. Discernment of the client's current stage of development is a major responsibility of the counselor, requiring wisdom and subtle understanding. Certain astrological factors, for example transits involving Saturn and the 10th house often indicate a need to emphasize social accomplishment and actualization of individual potentials. Other factors, such as those involving 12th house planets or outer planet transits, may indicate a need to become more receptive to spiritual dimensions of consciousness and existence that can radically change the person's conscious intention and life-purpose. For example, during a major transit of Uranus or Neptune, an individual may feel compelled to act in ways that others would consider irresponsible, unrealistic, avoidant, nonconformist, or bizarre. Nevertheless, from an astrological perspective the adoption of socially unconventional values, interests or behaviors may be "necessary stages of severance and deconditioning" that are prerequisites for the person's individualization and eventual transpersonalization.[21] The dynamic tension between social adjustment, personal fulfillment, and transpersonal metamorphosis gives rise to some of the richest and most complex issues that need to be addressed in any counseling situation.[22]

Astrology is one of the oldest and most venerable tools known to humanity for the guidance of souls. It is especially amenable to application by those trained in modern theories of personality development and psychotherapy. This chapter has described how knowledge of the birth chart can enrich the ability of counselors to assist clients in the pursuit of psychological growth, self-actualization, and spiritual awakening.

Potentials and Contraindications of Therapeutic Astrology

Before we can begin to introduce astrological perspectives into therapeutic work, it is important to understand the somewhat uneasy relationship that exists between the fields of psychology and astrology. While there is a growing interest in therapeutic applications of astrology, we cannot lose sight of the fact that astrology is still considered by most psychologists (and scientists in general) to be one of the last holdouts in modern society of primitive superstition and irrationalism. I can well understand the skepticism some psychologists feel toward astrology. For was it not the mission of modern science to liberate humanity from fatalistic, deterministic beliefs, rooted in religious traditions, such as those allegedly found in astrology? Science and humanism have tried to free human beings from slavery to the gods and to awaken our capacity to shape the world and ourselves through choice, effort, and free will. The repudiation of astrology was part and parcel of the rejection of the supernatural and seemed to be essential to the growth of science, reason, and a more enlightened society.

Psychologists often view astrology with great suspicion, for it may seem to be antithetical to their work of helping clients to strengthen their sense of personal efficacy and agency and to make their own destinies through concrete material, social, and intellectual achievements. A common view is that astrology promotes not independence and freedom but rather a passive attitude in which the locus of control of events is seen as existing outside the person in the planets. To a large extent this negative misperception of astrology is due to the fact that most of what the public knows as astrology is the Sun sign predictions found at supermarket checkout counters, next to the *National Enquirer*. It is also due to the tendency for astrologers to try to predict specific events instead of focusing on psychological principles and tendencies indicated by the chart. Another major problem is that many astrologers "read" a chart one-sidedly, emphasizing *information* rather than *process*.

This way of working with astrology is inherently disempowering; the astrologer simply interprets the information contained in the chart without soliciting any input or feedback from the individual. A truly therapeutic approach to astrology is one that explores the horoscope's symbolism through dialogue, not a monologue of psychic predictions. A therapeutic astrologer works with a birth chart in a process-oriented, interactive manner, jointly constructing meaning with the client rather than making pronouncements about the chart — as if the chart contained a predetermined set of meanings. We ask questions that reveal how the client is responding to certain planetary energies, for example a conjunction of Sun-Neptune in the 10th house. Without this kind of inquiry there is no way of knowing whether the person is already living in harmony with these planets, for example — expressing them, for example, through highly imaginative, spiritual, or service-oriented career pursuits — or whether the client needs guidance in how to better embody the potentials of these celestial symbols.

By engaging in dialogue with clients about the central themes of their charts, we discern their level of consciousness and functioning so that we are able to counsel them effectively. Counteracting the misperception that astrology is fatalistic, a therapeutic astrologer maintains the attitude that we can use our free will to shape the meaning of all planetary placements and transits. It is true that astrology reintroduces a mythic perspective, revealing the archetypal nature of the people and situations that inhabit our lives. Yet our work is to show the individual how to actively cooperate with the intention of the planets rather than to feel victimized by them and the dreaded fate they are often believed to foretell.[23]

Take, for example, the case of a person who has transiting Saturn entering the 2nd house. A traditional predictive astrologer might state that this was a sign of impending financial difficulties. But an alternative interpretation, and a more responsible one in my opinion, is that this transit heralds a necessary process of maturation that challenges the individual to stabilize her financial situation through concentrated effort. Dialogue elicits specific information about the client's financial situation that clarifies how well she is adapting to the developmental challenges, pressures, and opportunities of Saturn. To the extent that difficulties in this area are identified, practical suggestions can be offered. The same fundamental principle is true with any transit of Saturn. Practiced in this dialogical manner, astrology becomes not a fortune-telling method but a discipline fully compatible with psychology and a rational humanism — a discipline that can help modern men and women better their lives, make choices about careers, and understand their emotions, their past traumas, and their relationships.

It is somewhat ironic that while some psychologists might complain that astrology disempowers and weakens people's sense of free will, what they often prescribe is endless months and years of therapy, and, in many cases, dependency upon the expertise of the therapist! Therapeutic astrology actively cultivates a strong sense of choice, timing, and self-understanding. As we saw earlier, it is also a powerful means of quickly identifying central therapeutic themes and issues and can thus promote efficient, focused, short-term therapy. Moreover, astrology is a valuable tool for self-guided inner growth, which can provide alternatives to psychotherapy, helping people explore their inner lives independently of the formal counseling relationship and outside the traditional therapeutic setting — for example, through participation in inner growth groups utilizing astrology, meditation, and dreamwork, a powerful combination.

Nevertheless, psychotherapy is still one of the culturally accepted rites of passage for persons undergoing transformation — one of the primary places where initiation occurs for adults in our society.[24] Therapists are the most respected culturally sanctioned healers of our era, having replaced, for many people, the priest, confessor, minister, or traditional medicine man and woman. Moreover, psychological insights into the unconscious mind, family systems, the impact of early developmental trauma, transference and countertransference, and other aspects of the counseling process are now essential background for anyone guiding others, astrologers and spiritual teachers included. Many astrologers recognize this and have begun assimilating the important findings of psychologists into their work.

However, we must also consider the suspicion with which many astrologers regard psychologists. Many astrologers view their psychologist counterparts with a mixture of envy and disdain, admiration and mistrust. For, simply put, psychologists and psychotherapists generally earn more money than most astrologers and are treated with greater respect in our culture. Some astrologers feel some bitterness about this, for why should we not gain the same respect as other professionals? Nevertheless, I would encourage astrological counselors to enter the psychological professions both because of the difficulty of making a living as an astrologer in a society that continues to revile and ridicule our field *and* because formal therapeutic training teaches us to work with clients with a new depth of understanding and skill that augments the power of astrology to promote human transformation.

Undergoing clinical training offers us the opportunity to examine many central issues (for example, sexuality, addiction, family dynamics, personality types) that can greatly sharpen our work with astrology. I believe astrologers will benefit from embracing the study of psychology not only as a way to situate themselves professionally, but also as a way to gain knowledge and experience that enriches and expands their understanding of astrology and the counseling process. My own work with astrology has been deepened immeasurably as a result of my training as a therapist.

I believe astrology will one day be raised up to a position of respect in our culture once again and that it will be routinely used by psychotherapists and others engaged in the care of souls. In my opinion, practicing psychotherapy without referring to the astrological birth chart is like trying to study biology without a microscope, or like climbing Mt. Everest without a map. The birth chart is a uniquely accurate means of understanding the inner world and subjective experience of a person, and offers the most individualized road map available of the path of transformation.

Science, Initiatory Language, and Self-Study

What many psychologists and other skeptics don't grasp is that it may not be possible to adequately evaluate astrology strictly as a science. You don't evaluate a poem or a piece of music by the criteria of science, nor should we do so with astrology. I appreciate the efforts some people are making to validate astrology scientifically, but I am not convinced that astrology is a physical science. Rather, it is a metaphysical, contemplative discipline. Like alchemy, astrology is an esoteric, coded language of symbols that reveals sacred knowledge. It is an initiatory language, the meaning of which is understood only through meditation, and by those who become humble students of its mysteries. It is like the cryptic "twilight language" of Tantrism, which looks like gibberish to non-initiates.[25] And one can only become an initiate by reflecting on planetary symbols in a meditative frame of mind. Before attempting to apply astrology therapeutically to assist clients, it is important for us to thoroughly study our own charts. This involves a comprehensive biographical review, in which we examine the most important events of our own lives in relation to astrological symbolism. Only after we have become familiar with, and highly sensitive to, the character and activity of each planet, sign, house, and aspect can we guide others effectively.

Continuous attention to our own growth is essential to the practice of astrotherapy. That is, our skill as therapeutic astrologers is directly related to our level of consciousness as human beings. To guide other people, we need to know the territory of human transformation through our own experience. Through self-study, we learn to assume the centered stance of one whose purpose and essential identity are clear (Sun). We examine our own emotional issues, and become more feelingful, empathic persons (Moon). We develop curiosity about the world, read widely, and dedicate ourselves to continuous learning and exchange of ideas with others (Mercury). We refine our social skills so we are warm, friendly, loving people (Venus). We develop energy, enthusiasm, and motivation to pursue our goals; and we refrain from sexually exploitative conduct (Mars). Embodying the intelligence of both Jupiter and Saturn, we are both hopeful and sober-minded, optimistic and realistic, philosophical and strategic. We are able to set high goals and to work to achieve them. We are concerned with issues of meaning but also grounded in the real world.

But our personal evolution as astrologers does not end there. For to be true therapeutic astrologers, we must be committed to becoming fully evolved human beings. This means consciously passing through the tests of the outer planets and accepting the responsibilities of the transpersonal path. This involves meeting the challenge of Uranus to free ourselves, when necessary, from cultural conditioning and social norms so that we become individualized persons. It involves meeting the challenge of Neptune to rise above the illusions and transient phenomena of the physical world, to taste eternity and to touch the Sacred, through some kind of meditative or contemplative practice. This access to expanded states of consciousness helps us to become more intuitive so that eventually we learn to read a person *without a birth chart.* Finally, the transpersonal way involves meeting the challenge of Pluto to expose and expel the toxins and impurities of our personalities — such as resentment, hunger for power, and cruelty toward others. When we are free of timidity, awakened to transcendent dimensions, and purified of selfish or hurtful motivations, then we may be said to be proceeding on the transpersonal path.[26] Studying astrology to guide our evolution helps us to become poised and centered in the midst of all of life's many challenges. It is because of this self-study that, when clients come to see us in the midst of deep crises, we can find the pulse and help them understand what is happening to them.

A Container for Transitional Experiences

I approach astrology not so much as a science of prediction but as an art of biographical interpretation that utilizes celestial symbols to describe essential characteristics of human experience and to reveal the meaning of events. It enables us to revision, reinterpret, or reframe situations in the revealing light of planetary symbols and cycles. When viewed in the context of celestial symbols, even the worst defeat can become a sacred event, viewed and accepted as "a necessary phase in the ritual process of existence." [27]

Jonathan Tenney,[28] a leader in the field of psychological astrology, has likened the birth chart to a container or holding vessel that assists therapy clients through the breakdown and disintegration of old structures and the building of new ones. In his view, the success or failure of a transformational process depends on the ability to create a viable bridge between these two states. Astrology helps us guide a person through the liminal state — the state of transition between one way of being and another — by illuminating the meaning of this process and by revealing an image of its potential goal or outcome. The birth chart is a contextualizing tool for holding chaotic experiences. It helps us make sense out of what's happening to us, and what our current experience, turbulent though it may be, means in the overall process of personal evolution.

For example, a man named Peter had transiting Neptune opposite natal Saturn for a year. During this period he lost his job, he was unable to find other work, and his career fell apart. These events conform exactly to the meaning of the planetary symbolism involved: Saturn symbolizes the security of our life structures as well as our career, and Neptune represents erosion, uncertainty, and chaos. Peter felt as if he was on a precipice, like the ground was eroding underneath his feet. "I'm going crazy!" he'd often say. "What's happening? When is it going to end?" I explained to him that I didn't know exactly when this period was going to end but that this Neptune transit seemed to be related to what he was experiencing. I noted that it was going to last for another few months, so the uncertainty would probably continue at least that long. I also explained to him that during this period his professional goals probably would change and any notion that security was the primary motivating force of his life was going to be deeply challenged. Neptune's transit to Saturn was an opportunity for him to let go of old ambitions, to dissolve his fears related to survival, and to develop faith and inner serenity. I then identified a period several months in the future when Jupiter would transit over his Midheaven, when new goals and plans might begin to emerge for him. Most importantly, from an astrological perspective, while I wanted to know when Peter's difficulties would end and when his life might settle down and stabilize again, I was also willing to consider the possibility that this difficult period might have a *meaning* within the overall unfolding of his life.

This whole process seemed like it was perfectly designed and intended for Peter, as if he had to go into the Neptunian quicksand of uncertainty so that his awareness could expand, and so he could receive a vision of a different, more idealistic, spiritual career. In accordance with the general qualities of a Neptune transit, during this period he began to pray for the first time in his life and issues of faith became central concerns. He enrolled in a program that trained him to do spiritual healing, and when transiting Jupiter passed over his MC he did indeed find another job, in a different field.

On the outside this had appeared to be a period of failure. But ultimately these difficulties caused Peter to awaken to forces that were much larger than himself: the will of God, the presence of the Great Spirit, the infinite supply of healing energy and love. This transit opened Peter's heart, awakening compassion for everyone. This illustrates the other, often disregarded, side of Neptune's sometimes confusing visitations, which is to open us to the reality of universal suffering and the intention to be a healer of suffering. In short, this was a major spiritual growth process for him, even though it involved walking over some very treacherous ground. Astrology helped him contain his anxiety during this confusing period. What an astrologer can offer a person in such a crisis is not simply reassurance that "everything is going to be okay," but the awareness that an intelligent force is at work trying to mold him or her into a more complete, evolved human being. Astrology can be of immense value in such a situation because it helps the person find a center of calm in the midst of the storm, in the chaos of transformation.

Astrology, Meaning Making, and Choice

Astrology can also help strengthen the client's capacity to make his own meaning, rather than deriving meaning from an outside source, such as a traditional religious doctrine. By strengthening the capacity to make meaning, it contributes to the consolidation of the self, the sense of being a coherent, purposeful *agent,* one who is *able to act.*

For example, consider the predicament of a client named Jim with natal Jupiter in the 10th house in Aries and a natal conjunction of Sun and Mercury in Aquarius in the 9th house. Jim, thirty-nine years old, had a job he considered menial and was troubled by the fear that he might never find a calling, a work in life. However, a single question about a past transit helped Jim begin to view his situation somewhat differently. I asked Jim (in 1991) what had happened to him back in early 1986 when transiting Jupiter passed over his natal Sun-Mercury. Had he had some experience of himself as a teacher or educator? (Sun-Mercury in the 9th house of education, and natal Jupiter, planet of the educator or lecturer, placed in his 10th house of career). Jim said, "That's funny. That's right around the time my dad (a teacher) got sick and I got to fill in for him and teach a few of his classes. He let me substitute for two weeks and I got to be the teacher. And that was the highest experience of my life — the first and only time I felt like I knew who I really am."

That single memory enabled Jim to see that, as transiting Saturn was approaching its transit through Aquarius and the conjunction with natal Sun-Mercury, he had an opportunity to create, by his own effort, an identity, a structure, a work in the world focusing on being a very unique, unusual teacher. But he had to build it. He couldn't just have the unrealistic and unattainable fantasy of being a teacher. He had to work for it, to go through the Saturnian process of going back to college and getting his teaching credential, which he did. Having an image of this goal mobilized his efforts to work toward a new

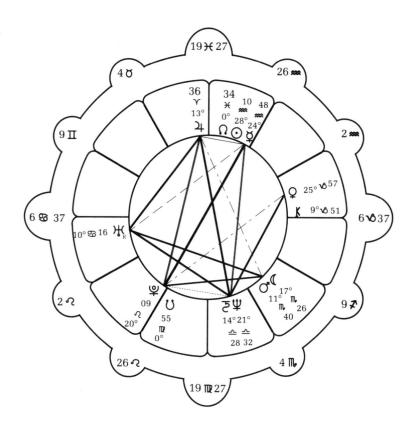

Jim
2/17/1952
1:27 AM
Los Angeles, CA

career. Astrology helped Jim move from a stance of powerlessness to a stance of choice.

Contraindications of Using Astrology

If astrology can be utilized by some to strengthen their choice-making and meaning-making capacities, we should also be clear that there are some people who do not possess the requisite ego strength to use astrology productively, or even safely in a therapeutic setting. It's important to proceed with the synthesis of astrology and psychotherapy with a sense of caution, because there *are* some contraindications of using astrology in the context of psychotherapy. One needs to use astrology with wisdom, just as one would not give a five-year-old a chainsaw or present an unprepared individual with profound Kabbalistic meditations or the secrets of the Tibetan Buddhist Kalachakra.

Some questions I ask myself when considering whether or not to introduce astrology into the counseling situation are the following: Does the client show evidence of avoidance, escapism, dissociation, magical thinking, or other thought disorders? If any of these are present, I would not utilize astrology in the therapeutic setting. Let us consider some examples.

A major problem area that alerts me to the possibility that astrology may be inappropriate is a tendency toward unrealistic expectations, in which the client gives over responsibility for his or her life to the planets, the chart, or the therapist-astrologer. For example, a woman fell in love with a man in a distant city who was married and had six children. It seemed quite unlikely that he would leave his wife and children to be with my client. She asked me, "What do you think he will do?" And I responded, "What are *you* going to do?" I could have done a horary chart to try to predict whether he would abandon his wife and kids for her, but this did not seem to be at all realistic. It seemed more productive to help my client face the situation squarely and realize that she would have to move on with her life and find someone more available and accessible as her mate.

A more difficult case involved a client who came to see me for a chart reading who, unbeknownst to me, suffered from multiple personality disorder (MPD), a very serious psychological disorder. When Julia arrived for her session I had no idea that this woman would report to have been raised in a Satanic cult, tortured, and subjected to very serious forms of sexual abuse, and that she had been professionally diagnosed as an MPD individual. Noting her Capricorn Sun in the 10th house, I began to describe all of her professional potentials. It was only when I finally stopped "reading" Julia's chart and asked some basic questions about her life that I began to realize I was not dealing with an ordinary person. It was then I learned that she had not been able to hold a job for several years, was on disability, and was in treatment for MPD. Obviously, these facts made me reconsider how I would proceed with our session. To examine her chart interactively and in-depth we would need to discuss the symbolism of her natal Mars-Uranus-Pluto conjunction in Virgo, which could be an apt symbol for the experience of violence and painful abuse. But Julia was not a person with whom I felt I could do this kind of work. This conjunction of planets was the symbol of

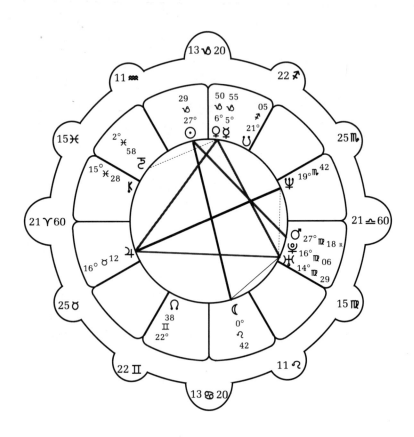

Julia
1/17/1965
11:03 AM
Los Angeles, CA

her most traumatic memories and highly charged issues and I was neither prepared nor willing to explore that territory with her — not being a specialist in this kind of highly delicate therapeutic exploration. Indeed, it would have been unethical for me to delve into this material with her both because she already had a therapist and because of my own insufficient training in working with cases of this sort. It is important to know our limits and to recognize that there are some issues we should leave alone.

Julia's story took me totally by surprise and I felt I needed to tread quite carefully with her. I didn't want to go too deep and to open up more pain, rage, and confusion than I was prepared to handle. Moreover, her thinking was so unrealistic that I felt astrology could even be harmful to her. She believed the planets were forces that made things happen and controlled her life. She also believed I was "channeling" the chart reading. In fact, I wasn't channeling anything; I was exploring planetary symbols. To explore birth chart symbolism requires ego strength and a subtle, non-magical intelligence that can comprehend the difference between a symbol and reality. She related to astrology in a completely fatalistic, deterministic way. Thus, this is a situation where I don't think using astrology is a good idea. Julia needed to do intensive therapy, find employment, and become a functional person. To her credit, she is doing deep inner work in her therapy and is taking concrete steps to help herself. She was also able to understand my reservations about exploring astrology further with her.

Another client for whom I felt astrology was contraindicated a man named Roger, who had a close T-square between Saturn in Cancer on the Ascendant, Moon in Aries on the Midheaven and Neptune in Libra at the IC. At the time of consultation, transiting Saturn, Uranus, and Neptune were forming a Grand cross to Moon-Saturn-Neptune from Capricorn: Roger was fragmenting under the impact of memories and emotional traumas that were coming back into consciousness. He was suicidal, depressed, confused, and unable to hold a job. Therapists use the term *decompensation* to describe this kind of psychological unraveling and deterioration. In many instances, clients I work with therapeutically are undergoing strong transits to their natal Moon, as in Roger's case. I see this over and over again. Yet for Roger, the process was complicated by the strong tension symbolized by the Moon's aspects to Saturn and Neptune. The Saturn-Neptune square indicated a dissonance between his highly developed imagination and intense spirituality (Neptune) and the responsibilities of being an adult in the world (Saturn). He wanted to be an artist, musician, and mystic but he refused to look for work even though he had no money and was in deep financial trouble. Roger exhibited many signs of what psychologists call "borderline personality disorder": major fluctuations in moods, dangerously self-destructive behaviors, unstable personal relationships, and innumerable somatic complaints. He was also unable to tolerate strong feelings without panicky feelings of disintegration (Moon-Saturn-Neptune).

Roger often asked me to look at his birth chart, but I declined because he tended to use discussions of astrology to avoid his feelings and his pressing, real-life issues. He tended to dissociate (that is, to space out) and hallucinate in sessions, and magical thinking was rampant (Neptune). He tended to look at everything in symbolic and mystical terms instead of facing himself and his life clearly and realistically. Astrology actually exacerbated Roger's feelings of not being a solid and real person and his tendency to minimize the gravity of his situation. At the same time, understanding the intense psychological pressures indicated by his birth chart did alert me to the strong possibility of decompensation. In this case, emphasizing Saturnian values of groundedness and greater practicality, and forging an enduring and reliable therapeutic relationship were necessary steps to assist this highly unstable person.

I would strongly advise against using astrology as a tool for treatment of persons suffering from any serious psychological disorder, such as MPD, bipolar disorder (manic-depressive illnesses), schizophrenia, borderline personality disorder, or severe phobias. For these, the treatment methods of clinical psychology are best applied by a qualified professional. Therapeutic astrology, in my view, is best indicated for clients with a relatively resilient, stable, cohesive sense of self, and who do not exhibit obvious signs of psychopathology.

Of course, there are exceptions to this principle. In 1982 I spoke with Wendy, a schizophrenic woman whom I know, hospitalized for many years, who showed some interest in her birth chart. While I did not discuss the chart with her in any depth, I noted that she was approaching her Saturn Return. I suggested to Wendy that she had an important choice to make: Could she gather the courage now to make the effort to come back to the world, to return to consensus reality, to become autonomous and able to care for herself, and to leave behind her identity as a sick person, a "mental patient"? I noted to myself that her 10th house Sun was trine to Saturn in her 1st

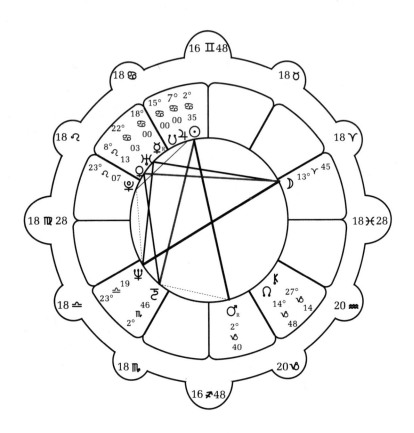

Wendy
6/24/1954
12:00 Noon
Baltimore, MD

house, and that she had Mars in Capricorn, sextile to Saturn. These factors suggested that she had at least the potential to become responsible for herself and even capable of ambition. Some time later she was released from the mental hospital. She became a born-again Christian and, with the support and assistance of her family and members of her congregation, she gradually grew more stable and developed a stronger sense of her strengths and talents. As I write this in 1995, I can report that she is currently married, working, and enrolled in law school. While astrology (and I personally) played no role whatsoever in her long, courageous process of healing, it pleases me to think that our conversation may have helped her, simply by planting the idea in her mind that even the planets indicated that she was capable of getting well again.

Astrological Symbols and Therapeutic Issues

As we saw earlier, astrology is a valuable tool for psycho-therapists because it can help us assess the kinds of issues the client is likely to be grappling with at a given time and the approach to therapy that might be most effective. Someone skilled in astrology can discern how long a particular process may be operative, and where the counseling process could optimally focus at a particular time: emotional catharsis, breaking away from the family, finding a better job, love matters, spiritual growth. For example, the current house and sign position of transiting Saturn always indicates an area where a maturational process is underway, attempting to make us stronger, more mature, and more sophisticated in our functioning and understanding.

Astrology teaches us that the pattern of optimal evolution is different for each person. This corrects the tendency in therapy to try to get the client to conform to a single model of development or a single goal state. Examining the client's birth chart helps us choose between alternative approaches to therapy and personal growth. This helps us work *with* the person, not imposing *our* models and theories on them and expecting them to change to fit our own preconceptions. Maybe the client's next step is one that totally contradicts our own opinions or ethical stance. Perhaps a client experiencing a strong Uranus transit decides to divorce, a decision that may make the therapist highly uncomfortable if he or she happens to be devoutly Catholic and vehemently opposed to divorce. Nevertheless, this might be the right step for that person to take. Perhaps the client decides to join a religious movement or spiritual community even though we personally view such groups with suspicion. Maybe we think everyone should do vipassana meditation or join a Twelve Step group, but a client doesn't feel drawn to such a path. Do we interpret this as "resistance" or do we work *with* the client?

Good therapy isn't getting the client to conform to our own image of mental health or positive growth; it's getting the client into alignment with the ever-changing *now*, and with the path in life that's right for them. Astrology can help us to discern, and cooperate with, the changing focus of therapy and the client's unique pattern of development. It also highlights the need to use different therapeutic approaches in different cases, and at different times with each individual client. It keeps us flexible, and teaches us to not get stuck in one way of doing therapy. Therapeutic astrology also assists us in working with the client to coordinate different levels of evolution and to resolve many different issues at the same time.

Astrology and Multi-Level Initiation

We are complex people, with many things happening at once in our lives. At any given moment, we are experiencing multiple levels of transformation. I call this the principle of *multi-level initiation*. Not only does astrology reveal the many archetypes, gods, and goddesses who dwell and live within us, our many-sidedness, what James Hillman would call our "polytheistic" multiplicity; it also addresses and illuminates the fact that human beings live their lives within *multiple narratives*, co-existent, interpenetrating story lines — for example, the narratives of the search for love and emotional sustenance; success in career; wealth and comfort; inner serenity and spiritual awakening. In a letter he once wrote to me, Dane Rudhyar made a comment about, "polyphonic, counterpunctual living." Here Rudhyar was evoking an image of a way of living on multiple levels simultaneously. Astrology is a unique way of coordinating our development on many levels at once, orchestrating our many inner voices, responsibilities, challenging relationships, and creative strivings into a rich, symphonic life. It is a tool for *multi-level counseling* — counseling that addresses and illuminates the diverse stories or levels of evolution that are unfolding for us at any given time.

Consider the example of a man named Dennis with Scorpio Sun in the 1st house square the Moon in Aquarius in the 4th house. He started therapy when Saturn entered Aquarius and was conjunct his natal Moon, and squaring his natal Sun.

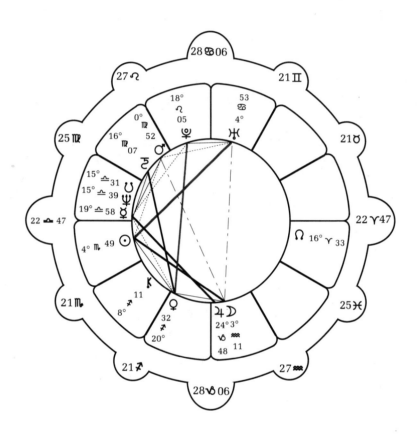

Dennis
10/28/1949
5:45 AM
Portland, OR

Transiting Saturn conjunct Moon (feelings, moods, memories) is a classic transit for entering the cave of depression that may both precede and follow the recovery of deeply submerged memories and feelings. It is a transit that heralds a major reorganization of a person's emotional life. At the beginning of therapy Dennis presented the following dream: "I am in our family home. I am six or seven years old and I am with my mother, and we are cleaning out the closets." This dream heralded a process whereby, at the age of forty-two, Dennis began remembering for the first time what really happened in his early childhood and in his family (4th house). Both the Moon and the 4th house are central to the therapeutic process as we classically think of it because they are both concerned with emotional memory. In the 4th house, in particular, we can gain important insights into the dynamics of our family of origin, the family and home situation that shaped us emotionally.

With transiting Saturn conjunct his Moon, Dennis began to recall many things. He remembered for the first time in many years what his mother (Moon) looked like, felt like, and smelled like when he was a child. He began to feel her moods and her unhappiness, and to feel a profound empathy for her. His natal Moon also squares his Scorpio Sun, and as a youngster Dennis exhibited very precocious sexual behaviors. While most children have some natural sexual curiosity, in Dennis's case this seemed to have been extreme. Memories of incest involving his older sister surfaced. He also recalled numerous instances in which he had been caught in the bushes with his pants down with little girls and little boys. For this he had been severely shamed, humiliated, and terrorized by his father. Dennis began to see how he had grown up viewing himself as a bad, naughty child, someone evil and disgusting. The message he got from his family was that he was not a good kid. In response he became ever more mischievous and defiant, developing a swaggering, tough persona to arm himself against the pain of emotional rejection. With his Scorpio Sun in the 1st house, his identity had become organized around sex and aggressive behavior. He had grown up into an angry man embroiled in a series of inappropriate sexual conquests with married women, obsessed with pornography, filled with self-loathing.

Scorpio represents our natural urge for emotional and sexual intimacy. But when these needs are thwarted, Scorpio is often expressed as aggression, hostility, or rage; the person attacks as a form of protection against an underlying state of emotional insecurity.[29] Dennis's primary pattern of response to situations was to become enraged, first and foremost toward himself, turning inward the aggression that had been originally directed toward him by his father. Dennis also frequently became hostile and disdainful toward anyone he felt had slighted him, failing to treat him with the proper respect and affection. With Mars conjunct Saturn in Virgo, he had a strong perfectionistic streak that manifested as extremely pig-headed, critical, abusive behavior with women. This was a repetition of the way he had been constantly criticized by his father. The intense anger he felt toward his father (Mars-Saturn) had been transformed into a more generalized anger and condescension; no woman was ever good enough for him.

More memories emerged during this crucial period of his therapy. As Saturn formed its retrograde conjunction to natal Moon, Dennis came to understand that there was pervasive, multigenerational incest in his family: His uncle had been involved with his mother, his older brother with his sister, his father with the family's housekeeper. He began to understand that he had been made the family scapegoat, the identified patient, the person who carries all of the pain, sickness, and pathology of the family and is blamed for all of the family's problems. He had grown up feeling that he was responsible for his family's misery. Now, during this Saturn transit to the Moon he began to gain some clarity about what had really happened, and about the depression that had always lay beneath the surface of his aggressive, macho behaviors.

Dennis also had a Mercury-Neptune conjunction in Libra near his Ascendant, symbolizing unrealistic and inflated (Neptune) perceptions of himself. He constructed grandiose fantasies of becoming a famous celebrity to compensate for his fundamental insecurities, yet he had never built his self-esteem on real achievements. His fantasies of greatness and his sense of specialness alternated with feelings of complete worthlessness and a recognition that he had never adequately learned to utilize his mind and his intelligence. Due to his poor self-esteem and difficult family relationships, he became unwilling in early childhood to do any schoolwork. He dropped out of high school and had never written a paper, used a typewriter, or developed any work habits or other basic Mercury skills. He was very articulate and could recite poems beautifully (Mercury-Neptune) from memory but was unable to write even a brief business letter because, even though he clearly had the verbal skills to do so, he was paralyzed with fear and anxiety by such tasks. He couldn't organize his mental faculties to get any work done. His fantasies of greatness were rudely brought back down to earth by the realization that he was a chronic procrastinator and had in reality accomplished very little in his life. He had never adequately mastered the tasks of the childhood developmental period Erik Erikson called "industry versus inadequacy," in which a child becomes industrious and learns a sense of competence by trying little projects, completing them, and overcoming fears of failure. Because Dennis hadn't learned these lessons, he grew up angry and mixed up about himself and his ability to complete tasks.

After transiting Saturn moved away from his Moon, transiting Uranus and Neptune started squaring his Mercury-Neptune, and Dennis began to undergo a new personal and spiritual growth process. Suddenly he became very interested in poetry, mythology, and religion. He went to a monastery for a retreat, discovered the mystical writings of Thomas Merton, and had an experience of the presence of God (Uranus-Neptune square natal Neptune). This surge of spiritual awareness was occurring at the same time as he was assimilating new insights about his mom's sadness, family incest, and his problems in school, and how all of this had affected his self-esteem. It was all going on at once, simultaneously. In the midst of these many changes, Dennis began to develop a more realistic self-image and stable self-esteem that was based not on fantasy or sexual conquest, but on appreciation of his genuine talents and personal qualities, as well as of his limitations (transiting Saturn square natal Sun). This example illustrates what I mean by multi-level initiation and the process of multi-level counseling, and demonstrates how we can use astrology to coordinate transformations occurring within multiple narratives simultaneously.

In a case like this, where a planet like Saturn is aspecting the Sun and Moon, the individual is going to experience a major transformation of identity and emotional response. Part of the work at such a time is to hold a tremendous amount of highly charged material and just sit with it. This aspect of the work of psychotherapy is different from what many astrologers do when they see a person once and send them on their way. A therapist has to process the client's emotions, memories, and pain; it isn't possible for us to take the pain away or magically cure the person. The therapist's role is to help the client experience that pain consciously, understand it, and resolve it. These are the kinds of counseling skills that a therapeutic astrologer needs to learn in addition to the technical capacity needed to read a chart.

The example of Dennis also demonstrates the insights astrology can provide regarding the timing and rhythm of the therapeutic process. When Saturn was conjunct the Moon and square the Sun, core memories spewed forth, the client entered a period of depression and faced defeats and disappointments that brought his underlying feelings to the forefront. During this period, he was preoccupied with memories from the past, issues about his mother, aggression directed against the self and others, and recognition of how his aggression was driving people away from him. It was an intensive period of psychological work. A turning point was reached when Dennis had the following dream: He was on his hands and knees potting a cactus plant. A cactus plant is a prickly thing that can survive and sustain itself in a desert with very little moisture. As he put it, "A cactus finds its juice within its own body." This became his personal metaphor for learning to live through an arid period of loneliness, and to find joy, purpose, and meaning in his own company, in solitude, without being dependent on the sexual excitement of a relationship. This was a very healing dream, for he *was* the cactus plant (Scorpio Sun in 1st house). A year later, Dennis had grown in self-acceptance. His work habits improved and he found a better job. He stopped procrastinating and started actively pursuing his goals.

Other Issues to Be Considered by Astrotherapists

It could be argued that doing a chart reading is itself a form of therapy. Nowadays there is even something called "single-session psychotherapy," which can at times be effective. However, generally when we speak of psychotherapy we are referring to an ongoing and sometimes protracted process of counseling in which the individual recovers memories, works through difficult emotions, and implements strategies for change. Moreover, a relationship is allowed to form in which some of the client's core conflicts are revitalized through the transference. To become good therapists, astrologers cannot rely solely on the birth chart; they have to learn a whole set of new skills, especially the ability to listen, not just talk.

Another essential skill for a therapeutic astrologer is the ability to use words judiciously and to phrase interpretations constructively, knowing how much to say and how much we should leave unsaid. For example, I once counseled a woman about to experience a lengthy, five-year transit of Pluto conjunct her natal Moon-Saturn conjunction in Scorpio. I grappled with the question of how to most constructively describe the issues she was likely to face during this period, without creating fear or anxiety. In fact, she went through a very painful, difficult period during this transit, including a divorce, a major illness, a dangerous relationship with a boyfriend who was a criminal and a rather creepy, sinister individual; as well as a confrontation with her own "dark side" — dishonesty, sexual obsessions, and cut-throat behaviors directed against workplace competitors. Working with this woman for an extended period taught me that using astrology in a therapeutic setting is different than just doing "readings" for people we may never see again. As noted above, an astro-therapist needs to be able to sit with the client through difficult material without trying to take away the client's pain. Therapeutic techniques like dream analysis and hypnotherapy are useful, or even essential, to complement astrology.

Therapy always unfolds within an "intersubjective field." A therapist is never entirely neutral and objective, able to perceive the client with unclouded eyes. The field of Self Psychology founded by Heinz Kohut has made great strides in understanding the therapist's role in creating difficulties, misunderstandings, and distortions in the therapeutic relationship. It's not just the client who does this through the transference. The therapist may be very uncomfortable with a particular client because of the person's race, gender, religion, physical appearance, sexual orientation, or personal mannerisms, and may act or speak in critical or judgmental ways that are very wounding to the patient, recapitulating certain core developmental traumas. A therapist who does not recognize this may blame the client for therapeutic impasses or difficulties, invalidating the client and inhibiting further progress in therapy. What some therapists might view as a client's resistance to treatment (such as criticism of the therapist, or wanting to terminate treatment suddenly) may be an appropriate response based on an accurate perception of the therapist's biases, limitations, or clinical errors.[30]

The truth is that we always meet our clients at certain crossroads in time that make us highly sensitive to, or completely *blind* to, certain issues and concerns. Here again the issue of self-study is pertinent; for awareness of how the client's chart and personal characteristics interact with our own helps us avoid these pitfalls and deepen the relationship into one that can alchemically affect both persons, client and therapist. Therapeutic astrology is a demanding yet powerful growth path for the practitioner; for our clients face issues we ourselves may be grappling with, and force us to face ourselves, including qualities that we may not wish to confront. For example, in my work with Dennis, his highly critical behaviors often triggered my own defensiveness, oversensitivity to criticism, and feelings of inadequacy. During periods when he was highly depressed, I had to observe my own critical, impatient, or hostile responses to him. At other times I myself began to feel sad and hopeless. Our countertransference reaction to the client often directly reflects the symbolism of some important transit we ourselves are experiencing. One day, while transiting Mars was conjunct my natal Pluto I started to overreact to something Dennis said, becoming angry and defensive. I immediately noted the connection of my inappropriate response to the planetary transit. This in turn enabled me to own my anger rather than blaming it on Dennis. For these reasons, it is advisable for astrotherapists to pay special attention to personal transits that may affect their therapeutic judgment and responses — such as transits involving Mars that might trigger anger, or transits to the Moon that might elicit a strong, perhaps misplaced emotional reaction to the client.

A therapeutic astrologer strives to provide clients with useful information, not useless, excessively technical, arcane jargon. We carefully consider what role prediction plays in our work and how productive that is likely to be in a therapeutic setting. By discussing the client's chart interactively rather than prognostically we can practice astrology in a way that empowers the client's own capacity for decision making and choice and is truly therapeutic.

In this chapter I have described some issues that need to be considered in introducing astrology into the practice of psychotherapy. I have touched on the question of whether astrology may best be viewed as a science or an initiatory language, and discussed the necessity for self-study, the relationship between meaning making and ego strength, and contraindications of using astrology in a therapeutic setting. I have examined some case examples demonstrating how astrology can be used for assessment, and determining the focus of therapeutic work, as well as how the birth chart illuminates the importance of a flexible approach and the necessity to work with, not against, the client. I have also introduced the principles of multi-level counseling and of coordinated psychospiritual growth, the subject of Chapter Eleven. The possibilities of using astrology therapeutically are only beginning to be understood, and promise many new discoveries in the years to come for those of us engaged in this exciting work.

PART II

The Planets and the Stages of Development

CHAPTER FIVE

Astrology and Human Development

To effectively guide our clients through the various transitions and crises of multi-level initiation, we need to understand the relationship between the birth chart and the stages of growth described by developmental psychologists. The field of developmental psychology studies the course of human life, describes the optimal stages of maturation, and illuminates problems, delays, or deviations from the optimal course that may occur. Psychotherapists determine what the goals and appropriate methods of treatment are based on developmental theories such as Sigmund Freud's theory of the stages of psychosexual maturation, B. F. Skinner's behaviorist theory, or Carl Jung's theory of individuation. Similarly, one of our important tasks as therapeutic astrologers is to correlate astrological symbols like the planets with various stages of human development.

Each planet represents not only a type of awareness or activity but also a particular set of developmental issues that clients will often need to address in the counseling process. One of the primary therapeutic uses of the birth chart is that it helps us identify which issues are most likely to be pertinent at a given time. In the chapters that follow, I relate the planets to some of these central developmental concerns. At times I will refer to some of the classic models such as Jean Piaget's theory of cognitive development, Lawrence Kohlberg's theory of moral development, and Erik Erikson's life-span theory. I will also note how awareness of planetary symbols can complement well-known psychological theories in some illuminating ways. It seems to me that each of the major psychological theories emphasizes one facet of development to the relative exclusion of the others. In contrast, the celestial language depicts the full range of multi-level human development. Viewed as a whole, the ten natal planets symbolize the coexistence and interplay of ten different developmental processes, often unfolding simultaneously and each necessary to the total maturation of the individual.

Development and Personality

Psychologists believe that each person develops a set of enduring characteristics known as personality. The course of development is seen as partly dependent on personality traits such as a person's degree of passivity or activity, introversion or extraversion, dominance or submissiveness, whether the person is trusting or suspicious. Five of the main traits that psychologists measure are *extraversion*: sociability, activity, interpersonal involvement (Sun, Mars, Jupiter); *neuroticism*: emotional stability and level of adjustment (Moon); *openness to experience*: inquiring intellect, intelligence (Mercury, Uranus); *agreeableness*: likeability, altruism, trust, sociability (Venus, Neptune); and *conscientiousness*: dependability, super-ego strength, restrained self-discipline (Saturn, Pluto). Many psychologists consider these to be the crucial personal factors. However, the concept of "personality" can be misunderstood to suggest that the self possesses fixed, enduring characteristics. I prefer a process-oriented view of identity as fluid and ever-changing, with new facets of identity and consciousness constantly evolving. From this perspective, personality is a term used to describe the predominant, recurring attitudinal and behavioral patterns that we develop in response to circumstances and that are always potentially subject to alteration.

The study of development assumes that human beings grow and change, that we aren't static and fixed. Astrologers especially need to remember this, for many hold the fatalistic view that the birth chart depicts traits that are permanently imprinted on us. While it is true that the birth chart does indicate enduring facets of character, we can learn to express the natal planets in new and more healthy ways as we evolve over time. The very purpose of studying astrology is to learn to change ourselves, to consciously express our strengths and to overcome or minimize our weaknesses. From an astrological perspective, the impetus for development stems from transits, which represent environmental challenges and opportunities, as well as psychological growth processes. Progressions of the birth chart also show how the imprinted structure of personality symbolized by the birth chart unfolds over time.

Nature, Nurture, and the Birth Chart

One of the oldest questions in psychology is whether our behavior and personalities are determined by innate characteristics or environmental influences. How much is our growth due to *nature* or maturation, and how much is it due to *nurture* or learning? On one side of this debate are proponents of behaviorism and social learning theory, who view experiences, situations, or external influences as the major determinants of personality and behavior. Evidence for social learning is found in the ease with which people's behavior and attitudes can be molded by conditioning, persuasion, or coercion. In contrast, theories of innate psychological traits contend that development is an automatic process of unfolding characteristics that are latent in the organism. Arguments for innate personality types include studies suggesting that babies show early signs of particularity of identity. Even more persuasive evidence comes from studies of identical twins separated at birth and raised apart in completely different environments, which show that as adults the twins seem to be remarkably similar in appearance, posture, personal habits and preferences, as well as in the timing of life events (a good case for the validity of astrology, by the way, since twins usually have very similar charts). Most psychologists now adapt the *interactionist* view that behavior results from the interaction of the individual's personality with situations. Innate, hereditary, or personality influences join together with environmental influences to form a constantly evolving self.[31] From this perspective, maturation of innate traits and learning of acquired behaviors occur together.

Astrology also adopts the interactionist view: The birth chart depicts the subtle interplay of personality and environment. The extraordinary claim astrologers make is that *what develops over time is a latent potential that is symbolized by planetary positions at the birth moment.* The way our innate capacities mature is by learning — that is, by confronting situations, symbolized by transits. But even if faced with adverse early conditions, the person's innate qualities (symbolized by the birth chart) can still unfold. Each of us learns and develops distinctively both because of our varied environments and because we have different sets of innate potentials that are trying to mature. That is why people with diverse birth charts respond differently to transits and their corresponding environmental pressures.

For example, each of us will react differently to a Saturn transit, such as Saturn's square to natal Saturn in our early twenties, depending on our personality traits and natal chart. Tim, a man with natal Sun in Capricorn conjunct Saturn in the 2nd house, felt quite ready to "grow up" and take a full time job at a bank at that stage of his life, while Rita, an aspiring artist with Sun conjunct Uranus in the 5th house, had more difficulty adjusting to the Saturnian social demands of young adulthood and could not hold a job for more than a month. But Tim, with his predominant natal emphasis on Saturn, had a difficult time when transiting Uranus was conjunct his Sun. He felt restless with his job and rebelled against his boss several times; but since he was not yet a truly individualized person apart from his role in society he could not envision any viable alternatives to remaining employed at the bank. In contrast, Rita, a more Uranian person by nature, thrived during a similar transit (Uranus square natal Sun), finding herself free to create her art and to express her true, outrageous self. The Saturn-dominated person like Tim may be very attached to propriety and security and often finds the changes that are associated with Uranus to be quite frightening. Thus, the astrological perspective supports the psychological view that while learning and environment clearly affect development, so do innate personality traits.

Our character and personality makeup determines how we meet developmental tasks and stages. People with a strong Aries or Mars emphasis in their natal charts will meet challenges related to intimacy and closeness differently than those whose charts emphasize Venus or the sign of Libra. People with many planets in Libra may be strong in relationship skills but weaker in self-assertiveness. Astrology contains many of these kinds of implicit insights about personality types. It also illuminates the fact that there are both *generic* phases of development that everyone experiences (for example, the Saturn Return at approximately age thirty) and *individualized* phases of development — indicated by transits that occur at different times for each person. For instance, Uranus can transit over our Ascendant or Sun at any age, and such a transit can greatly impact how we cope with other age-specific planetary cycles and their corresponding developmental issues.

Having briefly addressed these broad theoretical issues, let us now examine the ten planets and their relationship to central phases of human development that are likely to be a focus of our work as counselors.

CHAPTER SIX

The Sun and Moon: Conscious Identity and Emotional Maturation

The Sun represents essential personal qualities that develop over the course of time. From early in a person's life an inner light is apparent that gradually evolves into the conscious sense of selfhood and personal identity signified by the Sun. The Sun also symbolizes the individual's natural desire to be seen and *adored* as a magnificent, wonderful, special, talented person. Psychologists call this healthy narcissism. In childhood we depend on the reflective presence of others (usually parental figures) to provide more or less accurate "mirroring" of our identity, which reassures us that we are seen and treasured. This function of supportive reflection from others is signified by the Moon, which is the symbol of fulfillment of our emotional needs.

According to psychoanalytic theorist Heinz Kohut, the presence of this kind of mirroring bolsters our core sense of stable existence, efficacy, and self-esteem, while its absence tends to thwart and defeat the natural radiance and energy of the emerging self. If we receive adequate mirroring and we develop stable self-esteem, our normal narcissistic grandiosity can gradually be transformed into mature ambitions and goals and the Sun's energy can be directed toward socially meaningful projects. As this occurs, we experience a self-arising joy and playful creative spirit that is not wholly dependent on external recognition and validation. The Sun symbolizes the joy of being ourselves, of manifesting universal Being in our own particular way.

When a child is not accurately and lovingly mirrored, ambition and self-esteem may be thwarted, sometimes leading to structural personality deficits such as narcissistic disorders.[32] Symptoms of such a disorder can include an unhealthy need for attention, admiration, and praise; a tendency to use other people with no regard for their rights or feelings; or unrealistic perceptions of oneself — either grandiose or harshly negative. When the person does not develop realistic self-esteem and learn to direct energies toward attainable and appropriate goals, he or she may suffer from a lack of focus, a feeling of devitalization, or oscillations between grandiose displays and deep depression. The example of Dennis described earlier illustrates many of these dynamics. When transiting Saturn squared his Sun, Dennis became aware that he did not have many positive memories of being mirrored, affirmed, or lovingly adored by his parents. The lack of gratification of his natural narcissistic needs had led to rage, rebelliousness, depression, and inability to organize his energies toward achievement in school or career.

The primary goal of utilizing a birth chart as a tool in the counseling process, is to try to help the person consciously express the qualities symbolized by the natal Sun's position. The Sun's house position describes the primary area of life in which the person will best be able to actualize his or her essential identity, while the Sun's sign describes the root energy that the person will emanate.[33] The Sun's placement in the birth chart is the fundamental significator in the birth chart of personal identity. All our therapeutic efforts are ultimately dedicated to removing the obstacles that prevent the client from expressing his or her essential nature.

A woman with the Sun in the 7th house feels that she is most fulfilled through her relationship with others. Her life revolves around her husband and her close friends.

A woman with Sun in the 11th house is a sociologist who studies labor unions and populist social movements.

A man with Sun in the 2nd house is focused on efforts to accumulate wealth and achieve financial stability. Another man, with Sun in Taurus in the 1st, enjoys the security, comfort, and sensuous enjoyment that his high income affords him.

A woman born in 1904, with Sun in Aquarius in the 11th house, was involved in progressive politics from the 1920s until her death in 1995.

A man with Sun in the 12th house in Virgo spends much of his time in solitude (12th house) working (Virgo) at home and devoted to disciplined (Virgo) meditation practice.

A man with Sun in the 4th house in Aquarius, quincunx Uranus, left his native India to live in the United States. For the past twelve years he has resided in an unusual, collectively run (Aquarius) household (4th house). In keeping with the association of the 4th house with the domestic arts, he is a uniquely talented gourmet cook.

A woman with Sun conjunct Pluto in her 9th house has undergone an awakening of religious faith (9th house) as a result of a near death experience (Pluto).

A man with Sun in Taurus in his 4th house spends much of his time gardening and making improvements to his home.

A man with Sun conjunct Venus in Taurus in his 10th house is a professional sculptor (Venus) who has received public recognition (10th house) and good financial rewards (Taurus) for his work.

A man with Sun conjunct Neptune and square Mars is trying to integrate the quiet, sensitive, dreamy, ethereal parts of his personality (Neptune) with the side of him that is brash, energetic, impatient, athletic, and aggressive (Mars).

Brigit (discussed in Chapter Three), with natal Sun in Sagittarius, pursued her dream of traveling abroad and living the life of an adventurer.

The work of therapeutic astrology is to learn to coordinate the expression of essential solar qualities through the mediation of the faculties and levels of consciousness symbolized by the other planets, the Sun's satellites. The goal is for each of us to coherently embody and emanate our unique configuration of emotions (Moon), opinions and ideas (Mercury), way of relating to others (Venus), sexual nature (Mars), moral, philosophical, or religious convictions (Jupiter), and responsibilities and ambitions (Saturn).

There is a constant interplay between the Sun and Moon.[34] The Moon represents our feelings and emotional life. It also refers to the development of the capacities for empathy, caring, self-soothing, and nurturing of ourselves and others. For us to fully express the central personal qualities symbolized by the Sun, we need to be emotionally content, well nurtured, and aware.

The Moon is the symbol of many crucial developmental processes related to emotional maturation, a topic of great importance in developmental psychology. Psychological studies have shown that the development of primary emotions, such as joy, fear, anger, sadness, surprise, disgust, and then secondary emotions such as embarrassment, empathy, and envy, is due both to the maturation of specific neural circuits (in the brain) and to social learning of emotional behaviors. Studies have also shown that emotions and other behaviors are optimally learned during what are known as "critical periods." That is, if certain emotional responses and behavioral sequences — such as mother-infant bonding and attachment, babbling and speech, crawling, and walking — don't develop at a particular age, due to environmental influences such as deprivation and trauma, then normal growth and maturation are thwarted. While development may catch up somewhat later on, the person rarely learns this behavior or acquires this pattern of emotional response completely. This accounts for why certain people remain unable to bond with others or have difficulty accessing or expressing their feelings. Often these are people with "flat affect," who seem expressionless or unfeeling or extremely detached. Others are explosive and insensitive to the feelings of others. Stressful aspects to the Moon are often seen in cases of individuals who have suffered emotional trauma or deprivation, and who have grown up to be emotionally insecure or discontented.

The Moon also represents the mother, a figure of enormous importance for everyone. Mother is the root of our lives and our relationship with her nearly always has some lasting significance throughout our lives. We look to the natal Moon to understand the quality of the emotional connection between mother (or the primary caretaker) and child, and the kind of "holding environment" the mother provided for the child.[35] By gradually internalizing the mother's soothing, reassuring, nurturing presence, the healthy child gains a basic feeling of safety and security, and learns to sustain a sense of internal equilibrium. In an optimal situation, the mother (or primary parenting adult) provides what is known as an "average expectable environment," which means a physical and emotional climate that is reasonably attentive to the child's needs, while also providing the inevitable frustrations of some of the child's desires. The Moon's placement in the birth chart can alert us to the possibility of disturbances in the mother-infant bond, such as a neglectful, smothering, or harshly punitive relationship with the primary caretaker.

It is important to note that the goal of examining this relationship is not to blame the mother for all of the child's problems; nor is the actual person of the mother always accurately described by the child's natal Moon position or aspects. What is described, however, is the person's subjective experience of relating with her.

Lunar Aspects

The Moon's major aspects in the birth chart can reveal much about the nature of the mothering the person experienced as a child, as well as the person's general emotional state in adulthood. The person whose Moon is strongly aspected to Mercury may be somewhat nervous, high strung, communicative, anxious, or talkative, and these qualities may have been evident in the person's relationship with the primary caretaker. A person whose Moon is aspected to Venus may be serene, loving, and joyous, or emotional needs may be expressed through financial dependency or a hunger for physical touch. A person with a trine or sextile of Moon and Mars may be courageous, energetic, and enterprising, but one whose Moon aspects Mars by conjunction, square, opposition, or quincunx may at times be emotionally reactive, irritable, or volatile. These qualities may have been evident in a heated emotional connection between parent and child. According to Wisconsin astrologer Shelley Jordan,[36] Moon-Mars aspects are often found in the charts of people who express their dependency needs very aggressively, or who express anger as a defense when fundamental emotional needs are not met.

The person with a Moon-Jupiter aspect may have been parented by a warm, patient, encouraging mother, usually promoting a positive, optimistic attitude in adulthood. On the other hand, Jordan points out that with Moon-Jupiter aspects a strong sense of religious fervor or moralism may at times color, or interfere with, expression of emotional needs. In some instances Jordan also associates Moon-Jupiter aspects with exaggerated emotional responses and voracious dependency needs. People with Moon in aspect to Saturn may need to feel responsible and productive, and are often very serious, hard working, highly competent persons. The person with a Moon-Saturn aspect may have had an experience of maternal care that felt stern, restrictive, or rejecting, sometimes giving rise to sadness or depression in adulthood.

With contacts of Moon-Uranus, the mother may have been distant, detached, or inconsistent, or she may have been a very independent person able to nurture the uniqueness and individuality of her children. Thus, Moon-Uranus individuals may grow up to be somewhat detached from their feelings and fiercely guarding their freedom and independence. In some cases where the Moon aspects Neptune, boundaries between mother and child were fused, often indicating either great devotion of mother and child to one another, or an enmeshed relationship in which the child was encouraged to assist or rescue a parent who may have acted helpless or irresponsible. When the Moon aspects with Pluto, the emotional relationship with the mother or primary caretaker is usually deep and intense; in some cases, the mother may have been controlling, spiteful, or intrusive.

The Moon and Parenting

While we're on the topic of the Moon and parenting, let us note that parenting isn't all about lunar nurturing and cuddly warmth. It's also a *Saturnian* experience of being disciplined and learning to live within structures and conforming to societal standards.[37] The key is whether parenting can provide enough Saturn structure and consistency without thwarting the Moon's natural warmth and caring, that is, without becoming overly harsh. These insights are relevant both for understanding the developmental concerns an individual may have regarding how they were (or are now currently) parented, and for understanding the developmental pressures of becoming a parent (balancing the lunar, nurturing and Saturnian, disciplining qualities in oneself).[38] For example, Richard has Moon conjunct Saturn in Scorpio. He reports that both of his parents were strict, rigid, and heavy-handed with punishment of their children. When Richard became a father for the first time at age thirty-six (while transiting Saturn was square natal Moon-Saturn) he realized that he himself behaved this way toward his own child. He began to reexamine the modeling he'd received from his parents and did intensive emotional growth work in therapy so he could better handle his own feelings and avoid taking them out on his child.

The Moon and Emotional Maturation

As I noted earlier, much of my work as a therapist revolves around my clients' lunar issues, helping them reconnect with memories and unconscious emotional patterns, so that they can become more conscious of their feelings and their needs. Astrological study can help us recognize where our emotional reactions have become frozen into repeating cycles so that we can free ourselves to feel and respond less automatically.

Important periods of psychological and emotional maturation often occur during strong transits to the Moon. Some years ago transiting Saturn was conjunct my natal Moon. As the Moon governs feelings, memories, as well as the relationship with one's mother, this transit is often associated with periods of depression, regrets about the past, or problems related to the mother. While some of these things did come to pass for me, this transit was a rich and growthful period for me. I would like to briefly describe my experience not only as an account of an important period of emotional growth but also to illustrate how much benefit and constructive achievement can result from a transit that traditionally has a reputation for being quite difficult.

On an external level, this was a very demanding year of hard work and professional development. At this time my work as a counselor demanded a great deal of internal maturation and emotional growth. I should note that being a man of feelings has never come easily to me. I am a somewhat intellectually centered person and a bit cool, detached, and impersonal (my Moon closely aspects Uranus natally). During Saturn's transit to my Moon I was presented with many painful lessons about my tendency to be emotionally distant and remote. As Saturn fine-tuned my lunar nature, I began to experience a new willingness to honor and take seriously the feelings of others. Learning to feel, to access tears, and to develop greater concern, empathy, and sensitivity toward others was a major step forward for me.

The Moon is the repository of personal memories and also rules our emotional complexes. Thus, this transit triggered many feelings associated with family since my natal Moon is in the 4th house (home, family). I became aware that I needed to resolve some important issues with my parents, both of whom retired during this period. To my amazement, our family relationships grew warmer, more accepting, and more supportive. In large part I think this was due to the fact that I began to acknowledge my parents' importance in my life and to treat them with greater love and respect. I also moved to a new apartment, and spent much time arranging a new office.

When the natal Moon is placed in a different house, the memories, feelings, and insecurities stimulated will relate to matters connected with that house — for example, friendships and relationships if the Moon is in the natal 7th; career and professional responsibilities if the Moon is in the 10th; a desire for travel or learning if the Moon is placed in the 9th; political concerns and involvements with groups or political organizations in the 11th house.

At this time, I began to have problems with food and digestion, which are both governed by the Moon. I mysteriously lost the ability to cook, and everything I prepared tasted like sawdust. Food became less and less appealing and I often found myself debating whether or not to eat. I was also bothered at times by the pain of a mild ulcer. After some time, I recognized that my digestion was being disturbed by many strong and unexpressed emotions. I began to see that my problems with food and cooking stemmed in large part from a desire for someone to take care of me and a resentment that no one would do so. I came to perceive a very needy, childish side of myself. I did not feel taken care of by my partner and grew morose because I felt that she did not nurture me sufficiently. Over several months I learned the lesson that I needed to stop waiting for someone else to be my mommy! As Saturn neared its final exact aspect to Moon, I realized the need to make a choice — to continue being moody and resentful or to nurture and feed myself.

Yet paradoxically, as the Moon rules the principle of symbiosis, the experience of mutual dependence and support, I also came to accept in a new way the need to let myself rely on other people and to let others rely on me. This process was made clearer through my work with Jim (see Chapter Four), who complained that he had never had a long-term relationship but who believed that men should be totally self-sufficient, relying on no one. Tellingly, Jim's favorite movie actor was a man who embodied male freedom, independence, and adventure. Jung often noted that differentiation and individuation require an internal separation from the mother (Moon).[39] However, Jim exhibited a classic negative mother complex, in which his angry repudiation of the mother (natal Moon conjunct Mars in Scorpio) lead to an inability to form stable and enduring attachments in adult relationships. As he came to grips with how his carefully maintained freedom from attachments was associated with profound feelings of emptiness, loneliness, and isolation he, too, began to value the caring and support of the important people in his life. This important inner growth occurred while transiting Saturn was square Jim's natal Moon.

When Saturn turned direct and approached the exact conjunction to my own natal Moon for the third time I was very emotional for several days, crying a lot, full of sadness and fear. In short, I was a cranky, whiny mess. Then, on the day when Saturn was aspected natal Moon exactly for the final time, I was in a grocery store when I found myself able to calmly witness all of my emotions. I saw that I was *not* my emotions. I was reminded of the great Indian sage Ramana Maharshi, who taught a form of meditative inquiry in which we recognize that our true identity is not our body, thoughts, or emotions. Rather, he taught, our essential nature is pure consciousness, the witness Self, the one who says "I have this feeling, or this thought, or this body." As I fell spontaneously into the awareness of the witness consciousness I experienced a deep peace, fullness, and spaciousness. Suddenly I became emotionally centered. I was not trying to control or repress my emotions, but I was now able to steady myself in the midst of the constant fluctuations of my feelings. I could feel each emotion fully, while also remaining inwardly steady as awareness itself.

For me, this process of emotional centering was accompanied not by a cold detachment but rather by an internal shift leading to greater compassion for myself. I began talking to myself very lovingly, the way I have sometimes imagined my mother soothing and reassuring me. I began to soothe and reassure myself, as if I had an "internal mother." My mental and emotional turbulence subsided, and I felt free from the sadness and depression that had subtly colored my life during most of this transit.

Through astrological study of processes such as this, we can help our clients grow an interior Moon, becoming more nurturing of themselves and others, and more emotionally sensitive, grounded and aware. Transits to the natal Moon like the one I have described here are always lessons in emotional maturation, an opportunity to process feelings and memories and to more clearly identify our true needs. These are times to confront some of our underlying, core emotional structures directly. For this reason, people in the states of upheaval that often leads them to seek out psychotherapy often are experiencing significant contact to the natal Moon. The birth chart can be invaluable in helping us guide our clients toward greater emotional awareness, the root of inner wholeness.

CHAPTER SEVEN

Venus, Mars, and the Astrological Dynamics of Relationships

Many individuals who seek guidance from counselors have pressing questions about their relationships. Will they ever find a partner? Should they trade in their present sweetie for a newer, better model? Why is the person they once loved so intolerable to them now? Relationships at times feel like a place of refuge and joy, and at other times like a snare, a trap, a place of entanglement. Too often we do not appreciate or feel gratitude for the people in our lives. We complain that our parents, our lovers, or our children were sent to us by mistake. But though we may sometimes struggle to break free of these connections, there is an evolutionary intelligence at work behind the tangled web of our relationships that can be discerned through reflection on the birth chart, especially the placements of Venus and Mars.

Parenthetically, let me add that many people use astrology to bolster their fantasies of finding the ideal relationship or the perfect partner. We may give up on partners with whom our composite charts do not seem propitious, or with whom we share challenging, problematic inter-chart aspects. (A man who called me recently said he had just dumped his girlfriend because they had "incompatible Sun signs.") We may find quite unappealing the prospect of living with someone passing through the emotional crisis and catharsis of transiting Pluto conjunct the natal Moon. Surely this hysterical person could not be the form in which our "soul mate" would appear! Astrology teaches us that each situation and person in our lives is a perfect manifestation of the universal energies signified by the planets. Thus, the celestial art is not so much a means to find the ideal relationship as it is a way to understand, and value, the very real relationships we *do* have.

Astrological study can illuminate for us and our clients the complexity and difficulty of relationships, and the maturity and patience that they require. It can assist us in working through the difficult aspects of our relationships. It helps us know when to come together, when to hold on through tough times, when to travel different paths. If we are single, it helps us understand when it is best to lay low and attend to other concerns, or when we are more likely to meet someone new. Astrology teaches us to move with changing periods and phases of relationships, and above all to develop a sense of humor about relationships.[40]

There are a number of symbols in the chart that describe the individual's capacity for relationship. Most important are the sign and house placement of Venus and Mars, their aspects, and planets placed in, or ruling, the 7th house. Transits and progressions can help us sense when relationships are likely to begin or deepen, and to understand their changing seasons.

Venus, the planet of love, eros, and the heart, is crucial to understanding relationships. Venus symbolizes how we interact, what we find attractive or aesthetically pleasing, and what kinds of people we like. It represents how we relate to others socially and how we like them to relate to us, the quality of love we express and that is reflected back to us in relationships. Venus's sign placement shows our style of relating to the world and to others, a topic explored at length in Stephen Arroyo's book, *Relationships and Life Cycles*.

The natal position of Venus, as well as early transits to Venus, can reveal a great deal to the counselor about the development and maturation of the client's social skills. This can include early childhood material related to the person's experience of learning to cooperate and play with other children, and to adopt culturally appropriate gender-type behavior. Transits involving Venus during adolescence can be helpful in understanding how the person adapted to the raging hormonal changes and behavioral challenges that teenagers experience. For example, one man had a very difficult time at ages fourteen and fifteen when transiting Saturn opposed his natal conjunction of Venus-Saturn. He struggled to learn new social skills as he started to go out on his first dates. He vividly recalls how awkward he felt and how preoccupied he was with his clothes, hair, and physical appearance. An experience of rejection during this period set the stage for later romantic disappointments. Significant natal aspects or transits involving Venus nearly always necessitate attention in counseling to the person's experience of social life and relationships.

The evolution of the social, Venusian self is also closely connected with the planet Mars, symbol of the vital-instinctual self. In childhood the energy of Mars is generally sublimated into motor development, physical education, and competitive activities, whereas in adolescence Mars begins to be expressed through sexual activity. Significant focus on Mars in the birth chart often points to problems or fulfillment experienced in this area of life, and issues pertaining to sexuality may be an important focus of therapeutic work in adulthood.[41] For example, a twenty-three-year-old man with a Mars-Saturn conjunction had many fears and hang-ups about sex that he needed to talk about in therapy.

A fifty-seven-year-old man with natal Sun and Mars in Aries (ruled by Mars) came for counseling in a state of panic because he had lost his sexual drive. For the first time in his life he felt no desire to be sexually active. At the time, transiting Saturn was square natal Mars and his progressed Mars was squaring Saturn, both of which suggested that a period of sexual restraint and redirection of his vital energy might not be inappropriate. Instead of viewing his presenting complaint as a symptom of pathology, study of his birth chart raised the possibility that his lack of desire was due to the unfolding of a natural intelligence within him that knew he had other tasks to attend to at this stage of his life, other than the constant external expression of sexuality. This perspective enabled him to view his situation calmly and to allow it, knowing that all things in life change, including the tides of passion and desire.

Natal aspects of Venus and Mars are particularly important. Mars is the planet of self-assertion, acting on desires, and the pursuit of whatever person, object, or objective is considered desirable and attractive. If aspecting Venus, Mars ignites Venus's sociability and the individual is often fairly outgoing, popular, and able to connect easily with potential partners. As Mars intensifies Venus' warmth, such a person tends to be affectionate and passionate. These two planets in aspect comprise the symbol of romantic love.

Any transiting contact to a natal Venus-Mars aspect, or to the Venus-Mars *midpoint* can trigger an experience of love, passion, and romantic love. Here love (Venus) and sex (Mars) converge. Occasionally, if Venus and Mars are in a square, quincunx or opposition, the person may experience some conflict between friendship and sexual intimacy. He or she might want to become involved sexually with another person who might only be interested in friendship, or vice versa. Or sexual drives might overpower the capacity to form a variety of relationships, some of which are not sexual.

Major experiences of romantic love are more likely to occur during aspects of transiting (or progressed) planets such as Mars, Jupiter, Saturn, Uranus, or Pluto to natal Venus and Mars, or the Venus-Mars midpoint. Especially important are stationary periods of transiting planets that contact these points. The length of these contacts often times precisely the period in which we taste the deliciousness of romantic love.

The key is to understand that this moment in a relationship *always* passes so that we must then deal with other aspects of life. After the transit or progressed contact to Venus or Mars or the Venus-Mars midpoint is over, for example, our partner might be going through another major transit like the Saturn Return. Now the person with whom we so recently shared such a passionate, easy flowing sexuality might be pre-occupied with serious life concerns other than smooching and cuddling — concerns such as career, money, aging, creating a more stable life. That person might be physically or emo-tionally stressed, focused on some vocational or creative task, or in the throes of major decisions or financial woes, and consequently he or she may be less interested in, or available for, sex.

We tend to pathologize *not* being sexual, when in fact a healthy relationship involves a balance of passion and restraint. Relationships, like all of life, follow cycles. There are cycles of making love three times a day, and cycles of hardly touch-ing each other for days, weeks, or even months at a time. Times when partners tend to feel a little more amorous than usual often correlate with transiting aspects of Venus-Mars, Venus-Pluto, Mars-Sun, Mars-Jupiter, or Mars-Uranus. Mars-Pluto aspects often correspond to periods of intense, fierce passions that can also sometimes spill over into anger or resentments. Periods of deeper relational fulfillment often occur during transits to natal Venus or Mars from the outer planets, or to the natal Venus-Mars or Sun-Mars midpoint. When such configurations are not occurring, trying to force sex may seem strained and awkward — those times when it just doesn't happen in a natural, effortless way. Many people simply abandon the relationship at this point, in search of another Venus-Mars thrill. Very often people conclude that when sex cools down they have reached the end of the relation-ship, discarding their partner and looking for a new lover.

A wiser response is to use astrology to understand the changing dynamics of the relationship and to live through all of life's changes together with courage, humor, and faith. The two partners can gain greater understanding of what is happening for them individually by referring to their charts and current transits. Perhaps other aspects of the relationship are ready to evolve. Maybe it's time to put more energy into the garden, or practicing yoga, or pursuing separate, individual interests and projects.

Astrology can teach us to travel through life with another person allowing the periods of lusty passion and delight to ebb and flow, to come and go like the tides coming in and going out, never being attached to one experience at the expense of another. In this manner we learn to face life's constant changes without resisting, without expecting our partner to be the same person he or she was yesterday, last month, or last year. Life and relationships are ever-changing. We do not have relationships with static, fixed, and predictable entities. Each of us is an evolving consciousness experiencing the lessons symbolized by planetary patterns.

Astrology allows us to discern how we and our partners are unfolding; and it teaches us to cooperate with what needs to occur for each of us to achieve greater wholeness, even if this does not match our own desires or preconceptions. For example, Ralph was a twenty-eight-year-old man whose previously gentle and compliant girlfriend, Lauren, now had transiting Pluto conjunct her natal Mars. Lauren needed to learn to express anger and be less accommodating to others, even though this caused Ralph some discomfort. Knowing that Lauren needed to experience this kind of awakening helped

Ralph celebrate the emergence of her new strength and assertiveness rather than complaining or trying to suppress it.

To get the feel of some of the astrological dynamics of relationships let's look at some further examples. Bruce is a man with a Venus-Uranus conjunction in Gemini, who also has Neptune in the 7th house. Uranus is the symbol of freedom, of desire for experimentation and 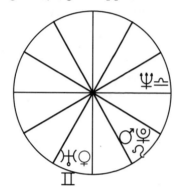 personal freedom. Uranus aspecting Venus may indicate a tendency to distance oneself from others, or an inconsistent way of expressing love. Love may emerge suddenly and with great excitement, but doesn't always endure. Bruce had great difficulty sustaining relationships for more than a few weeks. When he met women he emanated an aloofness, an air of cool indifference.

Venus-Uranus people need a lot of independence and freedom in relationships. In contrast, people with strong Venus-Saturn aspects may seek more reliable, conventional forms of relating, with serious commitment. Saturn is not a bad planet for relationship if you desire stability, continuity, and trust. One astrologer complained to me that transiting Saturn was about to square her natal Venus and wondered if she would break up with her boyfriend at that time. I suggested instead that she might recognize, and express to her partner, her need for greater commitment and stability in their relationship. I reminded her that Saturn is the planet of conscious choice. They were married during that transit.

Bruce, who also has Neptune in the 7th house of relationships, tended to idealize others. Neptune in the 7th house or aspecting Venus often signifies high and sometimes unrealistic expectations about love. If Saturn represents that which is most tangible and concrete, Neptune rules illusions and unrealistic perceptions. Bruce idealized spiritual teachers and also kept thinking that he had met the perfect woman. Then he became very disappointed when they failed to live up to his expectations. He had a long association with a spiritual teacher (Neptune in 7th) whom he thought was a perfect, God-like being. He surrendered to the teacher, serving (Neptune) him as a disciple. Then he left very angrily. Bruce also has a Mars-Pluto conjunction in Leo. Mars symbolizes aggression, and Pluto represents things that are hidden or repressed. He has much repressed rage that erupted when this teacher disappointed him. He began to badmouth the teacher, criticizing him bitterly. Meanwhile his passionate nature (Mars-Pluto) was not getting expressed, causing considerable sexual tension. It was a difficult situation. Fortunately, he knew astrology and worked hard to change himself. He also took classes in Tantra Yoga, which helped him break through some of his sexual inhibitions and become more confident. Ultimately, when transiting Uranus squared natal Neptune at the age of fifty-two, he married a very unique and very talkative woman (Venus-Uranus in Gemini), who was also spiritually oriented and a filmmaker (Neptune in 7th).

This example illustrates how astrology can help us actualize our fullest capacity for relationship, once we overcome our fears about our charts. Each of us can find a positive expression of whatever is in our birthmaps.

For example, another astrologer once told me, "My Venus is a total wreck. It's hopeless." The only thing hopeless was her attitude! She had Venus square Uranus and Pluto. She liked to party hard and to have several lovers at once. Considering the symbolism of her birth chart, this may not have been totally inappropriate. She needed to learn to stop judging herself and to value and celebrate the intense circuit of planetary energies that shaped her experience of relationships.

Brian, a man with Moon, Mercury, and Mars in Virgo in the 7th house, felt constantly criticized by his wife. Brian needed to learn to fight back, and as he did so their quarreling and bickering (Mercury-Mars) was transformed into more active, clear, precise (Virgo) 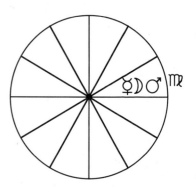 communication. They began to rediscover the art of conversation with one another. They also renewed many interests that they shared in health and the healing arts (Virgo), and embarked together upon a stringent dietary regime.

For Anna, a woman with Venus, Saturn, and Neptune conjunct in Libra, evolution of her capacity for relationship has been a major focus of her life. With Neptune aspecting Venus, she has sought perfection in love, and had a romantic ideal that she felt would never be ful-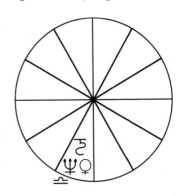

filled. Archetypes can be perfect. But human beings always have Saturn in their birth charts and, thus, blockages that need to be resolved. That's why we incarnate in the first place! Saturn's aspect to Venus symbolized how Anna's romantic illusions were constantly challenged by the realities of another person. Relationship after relationship ended in disappointment. Before she learned astrology she complained that she always attracted either stern, rigid, stuck-up men or dysfunctional, alcoholic, or drug-addicted poets. Where was her shining prince? As Anna meditated on this conjunction, she decided there had to be a way to experience the healthy side of both Saturn and Neptune, and in one person. She made up her mind that she needed a man of spirit, kindness, and imagination (Neptune) who was also a stable, reliable person (Saturn). She grew more comfortable with the commitments and responsibilities that relationships require, and more willing to tolerate another person's imperfections — their bad jokes, bad breath, depressed moods, unprovoked rages, jealousies, and so forth. Anna learned to balance the Neptunian search for perfection with the mature, adult attitude of Saturn, which teaches us to live within the limitations of form, and which gives us an anchor to the earth.

The chart of Peter, who has Saturn in his 7th house, trine Venus, and opposing Mars in the 1st house, illustrates similar dynamics. In his youth Peter viewed himself as something of a stud (1st house Mars). But, much to his dismay, he found that if he slept with a woman once he ended up involved with her for five or ten years. His relationships have always been long-term and serious (Saturn). Although he feared that commitment would restrict the free expression of his sexuality, he sensed that he was being asked to express his Mars within the containing structure of stable relationships (Mars opposite Saturn in 7th). Wherever Saturn is placed in our charts we make commitments that have lasting ramifications. Structures must be built in this area that can

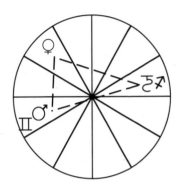

endure and lend our lives stability and focus. In his case this process operated in the domain of relationship (7th house). At the beginning of his Saturn Return panicked and struggled to bail out of a relationship. But on the date of Saturn's retrograde transit over natal Saturn, Peter learned that his lover was pregnant. By the third pass of Saturn over natal Saturn they were married. Now marriage is the center of his life.

Contrast this story with that of Linda, a woman with a natal Venus-Sun conjunction and Uranus conjunct her Descendant. With her Venus-Sun aspect, she was an attractive, affectionate person. But her 7th house Uranus symbolized a fear of being tied down and a great deal of

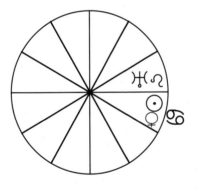

turbulence in her relationships. Such people may experience discomfort with too much closeness, find it difficult to have conventional relationships, or feel restless and discontented with enduring commitments. Long-term relationships are possible, but it's helpful if their partners give them plenty of freedom, regular time alone, their own room, or the freedom to have other friends.

At birth the conjunction of Venus-Sun was wide. Now they had moved by secondary progression into a conjunction lasting seven years, of which she was in the fourth year. During a progressed conjunction of Venus-Sun, it is likely that a person will experience an active period of romance, possibly even marriage. However, when assessing the effects of transits or progressions we must always refer back to the birth chart; and Linda's Uranus in the 7th suggested that she was wired for a bit of strangeness, instability, or experimentation in love. As it turned out, during the past four years she had already been married and divorced five times! Because of Uranus's placement in the 7th house, she didn't want to be committed to anyone for very long. This story illustrates the fact that we have to study the *entire chart* to understand how a person will experience relationships. Her story also raises the question (discussed earlier) of whether we can work with a client such as Linda without judging her or imposing our own standards and values on her. Clearly Linda had many issues about relationships and intimacy to work on in counseling, and she herself felt that there was something not quite right about the way her love life was proceeding. But fundamentally she did not *want* to settle down into a conventional marriage with one person.

Previous therapists had attempted to impress upon Linda the importance of Saturnian values of marital commitment, fidelity, and longevity, to no avail. I approached her situation differently. I recognized that the god Uranus was asking to be honored and appeased through Linda's search for complete freedom within the relational domain. I suggested that she give herself permission to be flighty and promiscuous, rather than fighting with herself — as long as she practiced safe sex and remained conscious of the risks of emotional damage to herself and others. She pursued this strategy actively for seven months. Then one day she announced that she was sick of this constant experimentation. She said she was ready for something different. A few weeks later she got involved with a brainy scientist with wild, frizzy orange hair, who seemed to be a perfect embodiment of Uranus. They evolved a very exotic, open relationship in which they gave each other freedom to explore connections with other people. They were very happy together with this arrangement.

Transits and Relationships

Transits to Venus, or through the 7th house, show the kind of relationships we might be ready for at a given time, the kind of person it might be with, as well as changes in relationship values or needs. When Mercury passes through the 7th or contacts Venus there might be a lot of communication, good conversation, a talk with a friend. With Venus we might share some pleasant aesthetic or social experience. When Mars passes through the 7th, there may be a stronger focus on relationship, more sexual activity, or some interpersonal frictions. Jupiter gives an urge for adventure or more intellectually based relationships. Saturn's transit into the 7th (or major aspects to Venus) tends to bring very weighty, significant relationships, and partnership becomes a major priority at this time. We might look for someone older, more serious, and interested in settling down in a committed relationship. During a Uranus transit we may change a relationship or break free; we may meet new and unusual partners, or explore unconventional forms of partnership. During Neptune transits we may be drawn to more spiritually oriented people, or a more spiritual, devotional kind of love. Pluto transits may correspond to relationships that stir up deep passion, obsessive lust, jealousy, or feelings of betrayal.

As we study our charts more it becomes clearer what kinds of relationships truly suit us. Linda realized that she wasn't a failure because she didn't stay married to anybody. She accepted that she wanted to be free in love, to have many lovers; and that exciting and not very long-lasting affairs worked better for her than marriage. Once she accepted this about herself, her experience began to change. It is important not to fight or judge ourselves or our clients. No matter what planetary aspects a person may have, there is a way to find fulfillment in relationships that is in line with the birth pattern.

CHAPTER EIGHT

Mercury and Jupiter: Cognitive and Moral Development

Mercury and Jupiter represent two related lines of development, those of cognitive and moral development. Mercury symbolizes the person's ability to learn, to think clearly, and to communicate opinions and ideas. Its natal placement indicates an area that occupies our thoughts and where our attention is often focused. For example, a woman with Mercury conjunct Saturn in the 2nd house (money) manages her company's $17,000,000 yearly budget and is constantly weighing various options for personal investments. A man with Mercury in the 4th house thinks about his family all the time. A woman with Mercury in her 1st house is a professional speaker and writer who often makes references to herself (1st house). A man with Mercury conjunct Uranus in his 11th house is a scientist with a keen awareness of social issues and many original political insights.

Mercury is the planet associated with cognitive development, the evolution of mental faculties that has been described in the most depth by the great French psychologist Jean Piaget.[42] Piaget contended that mental development results from the ever-changing interactions between the organism and its environment, which lead to progressively more advanced forms of thinking. When our minds adapts to an experience we subsequently interact differently with the environment. Piaget calls the process of changing our perceptions of the world *accommodation*. In contrast, *assimilation* is a process in which we try to make experiences fit our existing mental constructs. When assimilation is no longer effective — that is, when there is too much disconfirming evidence to support our present perceptions of an object, person, or situation — we must suspend our beliefs and reshape them. Through accommodation, we shift and adjust our mental constructs to better fit reality and to take in more of the world around us.

The natal placement of Mercury shows the cognitive structures and filters through which we tend to assimilate our experiences. For example, Mercury in Taurus is utterly pragmatic and unhurried as it considers any problem or situation, while Mercury in Sagittarius tends to meet the world in lofty philosophical terms, measuring its experience against its high ideals. Mercury in Libra looks for the most pleasant aspects of any situation, and always weighs its own perceptions and opinions against the views of others. Mercury in Scorpio is ever vigilant, searching for hidden facts or secret motivations. Transits to Mercury challenge us to accommodate, to change our perceptions of the world. For example,

Saturn transits to Mercury require accommodation to reality, becoming more mature, sensible, and organized in our thinking. In contrast, when Uranus contacts Mercury we realize that the world is not such a confining place and that we are free to think in new, unprecedented ways.

Stressful natal aspects of Mercury (especially to Saturn, Uranus, and Neptune) are sometimes seen in the charts of individuals who have suffered from learning disorders, speech pathologies, attention deficit disorder, or other problems in cognitive development. For example, a woman with Mercury conjunct Uranus was severely dyslexic as a child and had many problems with speech, grammar, writing, and mathematics. As an adult she was able to make significant progress in overcoming these problems, when transiting Saturn opposed her natal Mercury-Uranus. She also began to read new kinds of literature such as fiction and books about political science. This was a fascinating period of learning and study for her.

A man with Mercury conjunct Saturn in the 3rd house had a severe lisp as a child that he worked hard to overcome. As an adult he became a teacher and lecturer.

A woman with Mercury square Neptune has trouble organizing her thoughts. This problem caused her many difficulties in her education and her career, where public speaking and writing are essential skills.

A woman named Lenore, with Mercury in Pisces in the 5th house, was diagnosed as autistic as a child and institutionalized for several months; as it turned out she was not in fact autistic. She grew up to become a talented poetess. She was not a highly intellectual person, yet her mind was clear and serene and her voice was hypnotic (Pisces), which greatly enhanced the public's reception of her poetry readings (5th house Mercury). She said that many of her poetic images came to her in the dream state or during quiet meditation, when her mind was free of agitation and focused, rational thought.

I am not suggesting that astrology can be used to treat learning and speech disorders. However, it can help us gain new perspectives on the person that can sometimes enable us to view the learning problem in a different light. The parents of an adolescent consulted me about 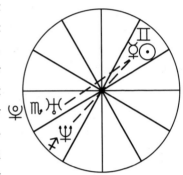 their son, Jeremy, who was diagnosed as suffering from attention deficit hyperactivity disorder (ADHD). Jeremy had natal Mercury and Sun in Gemini (Mercury's sign) quincunx Uranus in Scorpio and opposite Neptune in Sagittarius. He had a very active fantasy life (Neptune) and a talent for science and computers (Uranus). His mind was extremely quick and restless, and he had difficulty adapting to the slow pace of the classroom and traditional instruction. When transiting Pluto was conjunct natal Uranus and quincunx Mercury, and transiting Saturn was square natal Mercury he began to act strangely in school — defiantly disregarding rules and refusing to do his homework, which he said bored him. His doctor wanted to prescribe Ritalin, a drug commonly used in cases of ADHD, which can have side effects such as rashes, chest pain, headache, dizziness, and loss of appetite. I encouraged his parents to look for a special school that provided a non-conventional (Uranus) learning environment, accelerated curriculum, and skilled instruction for adolescents with special needs. They found such a school for Jeremy to attend and he thrived there, without need for medication.

Piaget has presented a detailed model of the stages of mental development that I associate with Mercury. In the *sensori-motor stage*, the child is aware only of immediate sensations, experimenting with objects and observing how they react to his or her actions. This process culminates at the end of the child's first year with the attainment of *object permanence*, the realization that a hidden object still exists even though it is not immediately present. The child now develops a rudimentary ability to imagine or predict the results of actions.

During the *preoperational stage* (from eighteen to twenty-four months to seven years), mental activity becomes conceptual and symbolic. The child acquires mental images, concepts, and words and becomes better able to talk and think about external objects and events. The child learns that words are symbols that make it possible to talk and think about absent objects or persons, or about past or future events. Internal representation of the world is still primitive, lacking organizing concepts such as causality, time, reversibility, comparison, perspective. The child at this stage is egocentric, incapable of imagining how things look from another perspective. But a gradual *decentration* of perspective begins to occur in which the child learns to view the world from the perspective of others.

From ages seven to twelve the child is in the stage Piaget calls *concrete operations:* More competent thought develops, including counting, classifying, and reversing procedures mentally. The child now also recognizes that external events have causes outside himself or herself. And in general the child is now better able to imagine how things look from another perspective and how others think and feel.

From an astrological perspective, the process of maturation involves numerous decentrations of awareness as each planetary function awakens. For example, Venus makes us aware of the presence of others — their beauty, and the ways they are different from ourselves. Jupiter awakens us to the broader sphere of philosophy, moral values, or religious doctrines. Saturn makes us aware of the institutions of society and the need to adapt to them. In each case, awareness steadily expands to incorporate something outside of the self and to make it a part of the self. Mercury's function is to integrate our thoughts and perceptions about these many facets of life.

The final cognitive stage described by Piaget is that of *formal operations*, which we generally attain during adolescence. Here we learn to think about abstract relationships like ratio and probability, to comprehend algebra, and to engage in scientific thought. Now we can now formulate a hypothesis, devise theories and examine possibilities, probabilities, and improbabilities, and reflect on the future, justice, and values.

This capacity to think abstractly is central to another important dimension of human development: the evolution of moral reasoning, associated with the planet Jupiter. Lawrence Kohlberg contended that our sense of morality evolves through six major stages.[43] Stage one is a phase of naive moral realism, in which our actions are based on rules and the avoidance of punishment. Stage two is pragmatic moralism, in which action is based on the desire to maximize our own reward or benefit, and to minimize any negative consequences to ourselves. Stage three is socially shared moralism, in which our actions are based on the anticipation of what other people might think, and their possible approval or disapproval. Stage four is social system morality: Here our actions are based on a sense of duty and the fear of formal dishonor, not just disapproval.[44] Stage five is a phase of human rights and social welfare morality or rational morality, in which we act based upon the values and rights that we believe ought to exist in a moral society. In stage six we define universal ethical principles, and morality is defined by the view that we believe all people should take toward one another. Thus, our actions are determined by values such as equity, fairness, and concern about maintaining our own moral convictions.

To see how the planet Jupiter can relate to these stages of moral development, let us consider the example of Ruth, a woman in her early sixties, with natal Jupiter in Virgo conjunct Mars and the Ascendant and squaring her natal Sun in Gemini. She sought counseling 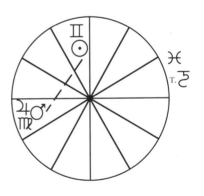 because she was having a difficult time accepting her daughter's values and lifestyle. Ruth described herself as a devout Christian who closely followed the moral doctrines of the Catholic Church. She felt that God would punish her daughter, Ann, for not attending church, drifting away from the faith, and living "in sin" with a man out of wedlock. She was quite concerned about what her friends and neighbors would think and say. They were all members of the same congregation, and in the small town where Ruth lived gossip traveled quickly and mercilessly. Thus, Ruth warned Ann of the disapproval and scorn to which they would both be subjected unless Ann changed her ways, returned to the Church, and married her boyfriend. Ruth especially feared that if Ann became pregnant she might even be expelled from the Church, the most dire consequence Ruth could imagine.

Over a period of a year, while transiting Saturn opposed her natal Jupiter, Ruth underwent a most interesting transformation of her moral sensibilities. First, she began to listen more closely to Ann's reasons for not wanting to get married at that time. She decided that if Ann and her boyfriend loved each other, wanted to live together, but didn't want to legally formalize their union that was their business, and that the Church should keep its nose out of their private lives. This was the first time she had ever questioned Church doctrine. Then she went further, becoming interested in a progressive movement within Christianity known as liberation theology, in which religious doctrines are the foundation for struggles of political liberation, rather than being used as a justification to suppress such movements. Ruth became a fierce fighter (Mars) for social justice (Jupiter) and human rights, actively lobbying for reform within her Church. Note that her Sun, which squared Jupiter and Mars natally, ruled her 11th house of political awareness and activism. This story illustrates a clear movement toward more mature, individualized moral principles.

Jupiter governs our desire for expansion, growth, new goals, a more cultured, educated perspective. A woman with

Jupiter in her 9th house (education) trine the Sun went back to school in her mid thirties after transiting Uranus squared natal Jupiter. She became keenly interested in philosophical topics, law, and ethics (Jupiter). She also traveled outside the United States for the first time, an experience that greatly expanded her perspective through contact with a foreign culture.

The interactions of Mercury and Jupiter, both natally and by transit, are extremely important. Jupiter lends philosophical and intellectual depth to Mercury's opinions and search for information. Piaget's theory implies that this kind of abstract, rational, logical thinking is the highest state of cognitive development a person can reach. However, it is important to realize that there are other modes of thinking, types of intellectual and mental activity not focused on linear, rational thought processes — such as imagistic, extrasensory, or mystical forms of perception. These are especially likely to develop when the outer planets influence Mercury. Uranus aspects to Mercury often awaken original, often revolutionary ideas, inventions and discoveries. Neptune's aspects to Mercury, on the other hand, awaken imaginative thinking, poetic writing, interest in metaphysical ideas, symbols, myths, and religion, or an expanded awareness of the infinite universe, the cosmic Mind. Attunement to Neptune leads us to stages of mental development far exceeding those described by Piaget.

The Cycle of Mercury

There is one further dimension of Mercury that I would like to discuss in this context. As a counselor I am often called upon to assist clients regarding their difficulties with studying and writing papers, reports, or personal creative writing. I often recommend that they learn to coordinate their activities with the transit cycle of Mercury. While many astrologers know the importance of the Moon's cycle in understanding the rhythms of life, very few recognize the importance of Mercury's cycle, one of the most significant and practically useful planetary cycles. Mercury governs language, speech, communication, writing, decision-making, information gathering, and mental clarity. Those who remain consciously attuned to Mercury gain the ability to function efficiently, to know when to make deliberate efforts to progress with reading, writing, and research projects, and when it is best to relax and patiently wait for new ideas, insights, and solutions to emerge (periods of what I call mental *diffusion*). Counselors can use the following information to help themselves and their clients plan activities requiring focused mental effort. This information is especially helpful to anyone actively engaged in writing or thinking. Knowledge of this cycle can help anyone overcome writer's block or difficulties with studies, and make more effective and accurate decisions.

Understanding this cycle can also help dispel the commonly held but totally fallacious notion that the period when Mercury is retrograde is "bad" or "difficult" and that no decisions should be made at such times. It is true that we are likely to rethink and reconsider any decisions we make while Mercury is retrograde. Yet, Mercury's retrogradation, like all astrological transits and symbols, has a purpose and intention that we can utilize advantageously. We increase our attunement to the way of the universe by living in accordance with all phases of Mercury's cycle, including its retrograde period.

I have found that Mercury operates in four major modes, which I call investigation, illumination, discrimination, and diffusion. Investigation is the process of gathering the data or information necessary to answer a question or solve a problem. Illumination is the discovery of meaning or a significant pattern in the information gathered, and its elucidation in some form of distinct theory, concept, or belief. Discrimination is the process of analyzing the solution or concept developed through illumination and testing its adequacy with discernment and precision. Finally, diffusion is that mode of mental activity in which we go beyond concepts and theories, let go of the critical eye of discrimination, and let our minds be unfocused and undirected — turning inward and in some instances contacting the source of consciousness itself. Regardless of which zodiacal sign it is passing through, Mercury continually alternates between these four modes of functioning during the different phases of its relationship to the Sun (as observed from Earth).

The transit of Mercury defines a cycle of mental activity that repeats itself several times a year. The most important periods of the cycle are when Mercury is conjunct Sun or when it is changing directions, turning either retrograde or direct in motion. Traditionally, periods when Mercury was conjunct the Sun were considered inauspicious as Mercury was said to be "combust" the Sun, and therefore its powers of thinking and reasoning occluded and diminished by its proximity to the Sun. However, while at such times there is often a tendency to worry, anxiety, and feeling overwhelmed by the busy, hectic, fast-paced quality of life, it is also possible to make important creative breakthroughs in thinking during these periods.

Mercury can be in two kinds of conjunction with the Sun: the "inferior conjunction" which occurs while Mercury is retrograde, and the "superior conjunction" which occurs when Mercury is direct in motion. During the period when Mercury is retrograde, at some point Mercury and Sun occupy the same degree; this is the inferior conjunction.

From the time that Mercury, while still direct in motion, slows down in the sky and then as it turns retrograde, some unresolved issue or problem begins to occupy our attention. This may be viewed as the symbolic 12th house or ending phase of the previous cycle of Mercury. Then, during the days immediately after Mercury turns retrograde, we begin a process of deepened searching for a solution to this problem. Remember that as Mercury turns retrograde, life seems busier and we often feel more anxiety and tension. Know that a solution or clarification of the issue will emerge at the right moment. Now is the time to throw ourselves into thinking about the issue, researching it, gathering new information, reading, and making provisional notes. However, at this stage it isn't time to organize our thoughts into a coherent or definitive decision, statement, or piece of writing. Rather, now is the time for us to simply try to get things moving and get our ideas flowing. I call this the period of *investigation*. For students or writers, this is the time to read, take notes and jot down ideas, not to try to create a finished project. This is the time to become focused on our task.

At the time of the Sun-Mercury inferior conjunction, our minds become clearer and brims over with ideas. I call this the period of *illumination* because this is the moment when flashes of insight or new solutions to the problem emerge into consciousness. It is the symbolic New Moon of a new Mercury cycle. What is most important now is to try to contain the intensity of this period by focusing as much energy as possible on tasks involving the mind: active thinking, writing, typing, gathering whatever information we need, and trying to shape any literary efforts into a more lustrous form. During this phase of the Sun-Mercury cycle mental breakthroughs occur easily and we can type, write, and think more efficiently than at any other time. It is also a period in which it is possible to communicate more clearly with others.

The sign and house placement in which a Sun-Mercury inferior conjunction occurs indicates the area of life requiring the most focused mental attention and effort at this time. For example, during a Sun-Mercury conjunction in the 4th house, we may put more energy into decisions affecting our home, domestic environment, garden, or communication with our family. A Sun-Mercury conjunction in the 9th house may seek expression through intellectual activity focused on a search for truth and meaning through study or travel. With the conjunction in the 10th house, professional demands require focused attention and new insight. One man took driving lessons for the first time at the age of thirty-four during a Sun-Mercury conjunction in his 3rd house. A song-writer experienced a burst of creativity during a Sun-Mercury conjunction in her 5th house. A woman reorganized her personal finances during a conjunction in her 2nd house.

This is a short cycle corresponding to some of the most rapidly changing tides of everyday life. At the inferior conjunction mental powers are at their peak. It is common to be incredibly busy and preoccupied with our own affairs. This is because Mercury's influence is so strong at this time that all of our "mental circuits" feel highly active.

This is not the same, however, as saying that everything will be resolved or completed at this time. Quite to the contrary, for the period between the inferior conjunction of Sun-Mercury and the period when Mercury turns stationary direct is a time of reflecting, reevaluating, reconsidering, reviewing all decisions or lines of thinking or analysis that emerged at the time of the inferior conjunction. I call this the period of *discrimination* because now we can edit, revise, and reshape our work into a structure that is fully appropriate for the task at hand. Now is the time to try to bring a piece of writing, research or a decision to some sort of resolution and conclusion, and to shape it into its most radiant expression.

Finally, when Mercury catches up with the Sun again and reaches the superior conjunction the cycle of Mercury reaches its symbolic Full Moon phase. Now we may presumably see the results of the new way of thinking or the decision that was reached during, and immediately after, the last inferior conjunction. However, since life involves continuous growth and evolution, new questions, problems, and decisions will inevitably emerge at the time that Mercury turns retrograde again, and a new cycle of mental activity begins.

Attention to the cycle of Mercury can assist us and our clients in pursuing the never-ending process of learning, developing our intelligence, refining our opinions, and expressing our ideas.

CHAPTER NINE

Saturn and Uranus: Social Adaptation and Personal Freedom

The planet Saturn is perhaps the most important planetary influence on the overall course of our development. If Jupiter represents our concern with defining some universal ethical, philosophical, or religious truth, then Saturn symbolizes the process of establishing a career, settling down, and finding a place in society. Saturn governs career development, maturation, and the stages of growing up or "getting serious" that most of us go through at some point. This maturation continues throughout our lives as we accommodate ourselves to the structures of society and the requirements of survival in the material world (Saturn). This process is most strongly associated with all transits of Saturn — for example, to the Sun, Moon, or Ascendant — but also with the major phases of Saturn's transit cycle, which we will examine in this chapter.

Saturnian maturation unfolds in constant counterpoint with the search for personal freedom and the expression of our individuality, symbolized by Uranus. Wherever Uranus is located natally, or by transit, the person seeks to experiment, innovate, or live in an unconventional way. The individual attuned to Uranus challenges socially defined norms and conceptions, often defying tradition and seeking independence.[45] The astrological interplay between Saturn and Uranus represents the individual's maturational struggle to find personal authenticity while also adapting to the laws and institutions of a particular culture (Saturn).

Saturn also represents fears and inhibitions, and its natal position (by sign, house, and aspects to other planets) usually refers to areas of life where we experience problems, failures, and disappointments early in life. For example, a person with Saturn in the 7th house may have experienced problematic or burdensome relationships. A person with Saturn in the 4th may have had struggles with parents or responsibilities to the family. Saturn tends to force us to confront certain difficult tasks and situations repeatedly until we master them. By repeatedly facing the issues associated with Saturn's placement, these areas can become a source of strength, stability, and confidence.

Saturn and the Father

Saturn is often embodied by the figure of the father, who, archetypally, represents order and discipline, the demand that we assume responsibility and conform to socially acceptable behaviors. Aspects to Saturn often reveal information about the individual's relationship with the father. In some cases where Saturn forms supportive aspects (such as trine or sextile) to natal planets, the individual's father may have been a solid, reliable figure who fortified the child's sense of capability and responsibility. However, other Saturn aspects can signify problems related to the father that can have enduring impact in adult life. Sun-Saturn aspects, for example, are sometimes found in the charts of persons who experience a lengthy struggle to gain confidence in themselves, often because of the father's disapproval. Such persons often work hard to overcome their shyness and fear of failure, to prove themselves, and to express their true identity. Stressful aspects of Mars and Saturn are often the signature of people with a somewhat tense, angry, discordant relationship with the father, who may have consistently thwarted the child's own desires (Mars). Yet if they overcome their sense of frustration or muted anger, these same individuals often develop powerful drives and ambitions and the capacity to become successful, commanding people, who carry an air of authority in the world.

Saturn-Neptune aspects are frequently seen in the charts of persons whose fathers were absent, weak, or a great disappointment; or who did not provide a sense of reliability, strength, and security. Thus, such persons often have difficulty developing a cohesive sense of self and a feeling of confidence in their capacity to cope with the material world.

A man named Lawrence had natal Saturn conjunct Neptune in the 6th house in Libra, and natal Sun conjunct Venus. Lawrence, who was in his forties, was still struggling with issues of physical survival. He was a gifted, self-taught artist (Sun-Venus, Saturn in Libra), yet he had never learned to earn a livelihood through his art and was hanging on financially by the barest of threads. At one point he enrolled in art school to learn professional skills that would help him find a job (Saturn in 6th). However, the formal discipline of learning the techniques of his trade

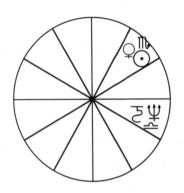

brought up deep insecurities, panic, and an almost over-whelming sense of weakness and incompetence (Saturn-Neptune). He felt judged by all of his teachers, who were never satisfied with the quality of any of his work (6th house Saturn). He took their criticisms particularly hard because they reminded him of the constant beratement he received from his father, an alcoholic (Saturn: the father, conjunct Neptune: alcoholism) who abandoned his family when Lawrence was fourteen — while transiting Saturn opposed Lawrence's natal Saturn.

Lawrence had never received from his father the stable sense of confidence in his capacities that any child needs; thus, he had grown up with a very poor self-concept and little trust in his abilities. With Saturn in his 6th house, he was obsessed with his failings and shortcomings. As he worked to learn the craft of an artist he tended to fall apart emotionally, becoming confused, distraught, and unable to cope, function, or work.

Reflecting on his birth chart, I felt that Lawrence needed to develop his Saturn function, the toughness that would enable him to contain Neptune's sensitivity. Thus, I helped Lawrence learn to steady himself so that he would not fall apart at the slightest trace of challenge or adversity, so that he would feel less fragile. I acted as a father figure for him, providing encouragement and expressing trust in his capacity to succeed. We identified phrases that he could bring to mind whenever he needed reassurance, and he allowed these positive thoughts to override his self-critical inner voice. He learned to master his anxiety and feelings of weakness (Saturn conjunct Neptune). And he became more organized so he could work with maximum efficiency in his craft (6th house).

Saturn and the Life Cycle

Saturn is a crucial planet because it represents our striving for achievement and ability to build the edifice of our lives. It is the planet of constructive effort. Saturn symbolizes our ability to work, to focus on projects and to bring them to completion, and to organize ourselves around attaining ambitions and ideals. To master these capacities we must traverse many significant developmental stages. These have been described with great clarity by psychologist Erik Erikson, who studied the process of development across the entire life span.[46] He perceived human growth as a lifelong process in which the individual goes through a series of psychological struggles, each characteristic of a stage of life. Because Erikson emphasized lifelong maturation I will use his model to elucidate the cycle of Saturn, the celestial body associated with maturation and the passage of time.

Erikson believed that the primary developmental challenge during infancy is the struggle of *trust versus mistrust*, in which the infant, through contact with the soothing, protective presence of the mother, develops an enduring sense of trust in the world. In early childhood, we experience the conflict of *autonomy and shame* or self-doubt. Successful resolution of this phase brings a sense of will power, independence, free choice, and self-control. During play age we experience the conflict of *initiative versus guilt*, successful resolution of which brings a sense of purpose. During school age (six to ten years) the child struggles with the phase of *industry versus inferiority*, successful resolution of this stage brings a sense of basic personal competency. Some of the most crucial events of this period usually occur at the time of transiting Saturn's first square to its natal position (ages seven to eight), which is often a period in which children confront limits, learn the consequences of their actions, and face punishment or rewards from parents and teachers. Early failures at this stage (usually in one of the areas of life signified by Saturn's house and sign position and major aspects) tend to dominate personal identity for some time to come in the form of complexes. Saturn in the 7th house or aspecting Venus can result in complexes of rejection and lack of social acceptance. Saturn in the 4th house or Saturn-Moon aspects may result in mother complexes. Saturn in the 8th house or aspecting Pluto may emerge as complexes related to sex, trauma, or violence. Hopefully any problems or fears arising during this time can be resolved during subsequent phases of the Saturn cycle. In some cases they are not resolved until the Saturn Return, or even later.

The next developmental crisis Erikson describes correlates directly with the next major phase of the Saturn cycle, the opposition at ages fourteen and fifteen. During adolescence, we experience a conflict of *identity versus role confusion*, through which we ideally achieve a more well defined sense of self. Now we come to see our parents and society more objectively, yet we often experience some tension between our desire to conform to institutional and familial expectations and the need to express *non*-conformity by conforming to the values, dress code, and speech patterns of our peer group. This tension is symbolized by the fact that, at the same time as the Saturn opposition, transiting Uranus sextiles its birth position. Adolescents struggle to define their uniqueness and freedom from social conventions and traditions, and often engage in the rebellious, wacky, defiant, and predictably unpredictable behaviors (Uranus) we associate with teenagers. This is the beginning of what, for some people, is a prolonged tension between Saturn and Uranus.

During adolescence all of the developmental gains attained thus far are tested. Mental faculties (Mercury) develop rapidly, and a new moral sensibility, a sense of right and wrong, begins to form (Jupiter). Sexual desires and behaviors (Mars) awaken, and our social skills develop (Venus). But most importantly, the period of Saturn's opposition to its natal position is marked by a struggle to achieve a deeper sense of discipline, personal competency, and self-confidence, and we often need to make important decisions such as whether or not to finish high school, find a job, or go to college. This is often a time of heightened focus on goals such as getting good grades and learning a greater sense of responsibility. Moreover, problems with self-esteem and anxiety, shyness and personal inhibitions are at a peak during adolescence.

To make matters more complicated, during adolescence we may also experience the awakening of the Neptune function, often through the tendency to fantasize, daydream, or to engage in drug and alcohol use. In some cases there may be an early spiritual awakening, and exaggerated forms of religiosity or moral fervor are not uncommon at this time, which corresponds to Neptune's semi-sextile to its natal position.

As we move from adolescence into early adulthood, a new developmental challenge is faced, which Erikson calls *intimacy versus isolation*, in which the ultimate goal is to feel secure in the love of another person. Erikson's model is somewhat incomplete in its description of this stage of development, yet we can gain some additional insights into the pressures and struggles of early adulthood by considering the astrological perspective. At ages twenty-one and twenty-two we simultaneously experience major phases in the cycles of two important planets, Saturn and Uranus. Saturn forms its third quarter square at this time while Uranus is now in its opening square to its birth position. On the one hand, this is a period of striving to create a provisional structure of adulthood (Saturn square natal Saturn).[47] This is usually a period of grappling with issues of survival, employment, living within the structures imposed by jobs and new responsibilities such as marriage or child-rearing. It is time to grow up, to be an adult, and to function within society. As we begin to be self-supporting, we may also need to separate from our peer group to some extent and to stand alone, sometimes resulting in isolation. Dave (see page 75) went into retreat at this stage of his life and stood alone, pursuing a personal quest that his friends did not understand. As Erikson has correctly observed, a major task now is to establish stable emotional relationships; without these one will surely experience loneliness.

On the other hand, due to the transit of Uranus, some people in our culture also strive at this time to achieve emancipation (Uranus) from parental control, to create their own lives separate from the values, expectations, and demands of their parents and society (Saturn). I view this period as one often marked by issues of *responsibility versus rebellion*. A major question now is how to fit in and survive in the world (Saturn) without losing our individuality, originality, and uniqueness (Uranus). Of course, most young adults are more attuned to Saturn than to Uranus and are consequently focused on the tasks of starting a career and finding a place in society. However, the influence of Uranus is always present, even if not consciously acknowledged. Thus, some people who adapt to societal structures by finding full-time employment, continuing their education, or starting families may experience considerable inner tension and dissatisfaction at this stage of life if they sense that their responsibilities do not allow some essential part of themselves to be lived or expressed. Others, responding strongly to the influence of Uranus, may attempt to remain free from rigid social structures such as a nine-to-five job, working part-time or pursuing highly unusual jobs and lifestyles. For example, some individuals at this stage might become gypsy poets or musicians, roaming "deadheads," or chronically unemployed "slackers." These are persons searching for alternative identities who may resist being absorbed into the mainstream culture and seek ways of sustaining their youthful idealism and desire for freedom.

Those who attempt to liberate themselves from cultural norms and pursue unconventional lifestyles often grapple with the feeling that they are socially marginal and may wish to better accommodate themselves to society and to become more culturally adapted by pursuing new careers, returning to school, or starting a family. Very often, this process culminates with major decisions made when Saturn returns to its birth position between ages twenty-eight and thirty (the Saturn Return). At this time, Uranus-sensitive individuals can become more stable, learning to fulfill the Saturnian requirements of survival without sacrificing their resolute commitment to following their own, unusual paths.

For example, Lance spent most of his twenties working part-time in a bakery, playing the flute, and learning various healing arts. At the age of twenty-nine he started to become aware that all of his clothes were full of holes and his musical career was not progressing, yet he consistently got rave reviews from his friends for his free-form bodywork sessions. During his Saturn Return, Lance made the decision to attend chiropractic school, which would enable him to develop a profession that was in line with his interests in healing, and that would give him the financial security to keep pursuing music.

The Saturn Return is a time to make mature, informed choices and commitments that will give our lives focus and stability. This transit represents the real transition into adulthood, the beginning of the cycle of true productivity in society.[48] We begin to live within new limits and new structures that define our existence for many years to come.

The critical question is whether our choices now reflect an adaptation to society that is in line with our personal inclinations and interests, or whether we are relinquishing our individuality to conform to the institutions, norms, and attitudes of our society. This is a time of potential integration of both the Uranus and Saturn impulses: the urge to be free and the urge to settle down. During the Saturn Return we can emerge as consciously individualized persons, functioning effectively within our particular culture, yet with a clear sense of our personal talents, our true identity, and our creative vocation. Because transiting Uranus has reached the trine to its birth position at this age, whatever is most unique in us can now begin to manifest (Saturn) in the world. But this can only occur if we possess both the Uranian boldness to pursue our own path *and* the Saturnian maturity needed to survive in our cultural environment. Thus, the period between ages twenty-eight and thirty is a critical juncture determining our ability to be both socialized and individualized persons.

At age thirty-six, while Saturn squares its birth position, we take further steps to distinguish and express our true identity while functioning in society. We begin to yearn for more stable, lasting life structures (job, home, relationship) as we grow more mature, become more aware of our aging, and witness the aging or death of parents. This is the stage that Daniel Levinson calls *becoming one's own man or one's own woman*.[49] Sometimes this may require repudiating some prior job position, relationship, or position of deference with respect to a teacher or mentor. We make strategic choices now that enable us to feel a sense of true progress in our career and advancement toward personal goals.

During the mid-life crisis period of ages forty to forty-five the cycles of Saturn and Uranus interconnect again, resulting in one of life's most dramatic phases. Saturn has now reached its second opposition to its birth position while Uranus opposes its natal position. Because of the Saturn opposition we may experience fulfillment and advancement, or a period of frustration, setbacks, or dissatisfaction in our work or relationships. By this stage we may well be on the way toward actualizing our dreams. Yet, this is also a period of major reevaluation in which we weigh our own goals, values, and ambitions against the expectations of our family, peer group, or society. Because of the Uranus opposition, we may now feel an increasing tension between social and family responsibilities and a desire to make a new start in a different, more independent direction. I call this the developmental conflict of *freedom versus frustration.* We question whatever is inhibiting the expression of our uniqueness and true identity, and a revolt against our responsibilities may take place — resulting in the career changes and divorces that sometimes occur now. This can also be a highly productive period in which our creative powers fully emerge. Richard Tarnas has documented the emergence and expression of personal genius, brilliance, and originality during the Uranus opposition in the lives of many great thinkers, artists, and scientists.[50]

The ages of forty-four to fifty-nine between the second Saturn opposition and the second Saturn Return, are when our most enduring structures and accomplishments are built, through sustained effort and commitment. However, as Alexander Ruperti has pointed out, if the gap between our ideals and the reality of our life is too great, we may give up in defeat and resignation to collective norms.[51] A sense of fulfillment or a crisis may ensue as children grow up and move away, as child-bearing years end, and as physical vitality diminishes. Responsibilities to job or family or our own life's work usually predominate, and our desire to make a positive social contribution may be strongest now. Alternatively, we may feel defeated by our lack of social advancement or meaningful accomplishment. Nevertheless, there is still time to make a new start through a major job change, new business ventures, or creative activities. What Saturn asks at this time is that our actions are strategic and well planned, that we build the structures now within which we can grow older, and that we gain a sense of satisfaction with our life's accomplishments.

According to Erikson, the period of middle adulthood focuses on a struggle of *generativity versus stagnation* — in which we seek to express caring for others and to make a lasting contribution for future generations, and that may also assure our immortality. In particular, the period between ages fifty-six and sixty, corresponding to the second Saturn Return and the waning trine of Uranus is a crucial time of productivity and creativity. In some cases Saturn's second return corresponds to a peak of social authority, achievement, and recognition in society. One may gain a new sense of stature and prominence in one's field. Others become aware of fatigue and look forward to retirement. In either event, we become aware now that we are truly growing older and need to focus our thoughts and attention on higher matters — whether defined in religious, philosophical, ethical, or mystical terms. We begin now to search for a frame of reference and source of meaning that transcends our particular life story, accomplishments, and identity. The lesson of Saturn is that each moment is precious. In ancient India this was the time to retire from the world of ambition and striving and to devote oneself to meditation and spiritual life. Having achieved our individuals goals and fulfilled our social responsibilities, we can begin to quiet down now and embark upon the inner quest, a path of meditation, contemplation, or artistic exploration. What is most important is that we begin to view life from a perspective beyond that of personal ambition and social status.

After the second Saturn Return at about age fifty-nine, the processes of aging may become a more constant focus of our attention. The challenge now is to witness physical decline, retirement, and the death of spouse and friends with equanimity, accepting change peacefully. The Saturn square of age sixty-five to sixty-six is often a crisis as we struggle to move toward the fulfillment of our remaining goals. The opposition at ages seventy-three and seventy-four may mark a climax — reconciliation with our lives and with others, or deeply entrenched feelings of anguish or failure. Though our powers may be beginning to weaken now, this is a time when true maturity is won and displayed. Physical brittleness may begin to be a reality at this time, yet the wisdom we have harvested from a full life gives us new strength to go on.

Persons who live wakefully until the Uranus Return at age eighty-four and the third Saturn Return at ages eighty-eight to ninety, have the potential to stand in the world as embodiments of transformation, holding the values of prior generations in their memory and experience. These wise elders can remind us of where we come from, our roots and origins, the voices of our ancestors. They are strong in their convictions, though they must often live quietly and self-contained while those younger and less wise rule the day. This is the time to witness the dance of life peacefully, like a panther content to lie completely still in the shade on a summer's morning.

Uranus: The Space Beyond Saturn

If we pass successfully through each major developmental stage represented by Saturn's transit cycle we achieve integration into our society. Yet we have also seen that at any stage of life, the influence of Uranus can fill us with an urge for freedom and rebellion. While we may exhibit some socially maladaptive behaviors, interests, or impulses at such times, our unusual, often controversial pursuits also represent potential social, intellectual, moral, or artistic breakthroughs that may one day influence the culture at large. In such a case, our adaptation to society (Saturn) is accompanied by a feeling that our personal lives are making a creative contribution to societal betterment and cultural evolution. Each conscious person who responds to the developmental challenges of Uranus and becomes a free individual helps humanity move forward by breaking through the mental conditioning of tradition and reinventing the world. Such a person may envision political liberation and freedom from oppression, or may discover new technologies to better solve problems and serve human and planetary needs. The Uranian individual can be an artistic genius who breaks with precedent and defines a unique style, or a person trying to apply progressive values to raising a child or earning a livelihood independently through self-employment.

The lesson of Uranus is that there is free space out beyond Saturn. We can create new structures, new values, new self-invented social roles. Uranus is freedom from cultural conditioning and the power to discover. Uranus-sensitive individuals are the seed men and women whose lives reveal glimpses of the future. Of course, when we respond to Uranus there is always a danger of exile, ridicule, or social exclusion. But there is also an exhilaration that comes from taking risks, challenging assumptions, making our own way, and displaying our inventiveness. We can do so productively if we find the right mixture of the adventurous, innovative spirit of Uranus and Saturn's pragmatism, respect for social institutions, and sound survival instincts.

While transiting Uranus squared his natal Sun, Dr. Jackson, a respected physician, was faced with a profound dilemma. His true interests were increasingly in the direction of herbal medicine, homeopathy, and other alternative forms of treatment. His colleagues urged him to "return to reality" and stop entertaining these preposterous ideas. If nothing else, they advised, he should protect his reputation by not associating himself publicly with "kooks," "quacks," and "fringe elements" of society. Although his new medical practices were shocking to his colleagues, Dr. Jackson knew that to be true to himself he had to keep pursuing these interests. He challenged the inflexible (Saturn) mindset and doctrines of his profession and spoke up at large meetings and conferences about the need to reform Western medicine to include a more holistic perspective. These actions generated much controversy. Yet

Dr. Jackson was filled with excitement because he knew he was participating in a trend that in the long run would transform society and medicine. He remained an active participant in his professional associations, practiced medicine responsibly, and demonstrated his results in a scientifically sound manner. As a result, a few of his colleagues began to listen to him and to incorporate some of his views and findings. As we respond to Uranus, our developmental focus changes from simply adapting to the world in which we live to a concern with how our actions can *transform* the world. The lesson of Uranus is that we are the instruments through which the world can be renewed.

CHAPTER TEN

Neptune, Pluto, and Transpersonal Stages of Development

In the last chapter we saw how Uranus inspires us to innovate and individualize in order to serve the evolution of humanity. The individual at this level of consciousness receives inspiration for experiments and discoveries with a more than personal significance. Uranus represents the beginning of the transition beyond ego. The individual begins to be electrified by the power of the universe, inspired by the universal mind and the spirit of invention. With Neptune we reach a stage when we transcend the physical and mental limitations of ego-centered awareness and begin to experience our limitlessness. Neptune awakens new faculties of consciousness and draws us farther into transpersonal stages of development.

In preceding chapters we have seen that, in addition to the need for fulfillment in love, sex, and relationships (Venus and Mars), emotional contentment (Moon), and development of mental acuity and intellectual depth (Mercury and Jupiter), two primary developmental challenges are to achieve stability within the social order (Saturn) and freedom to express our individuality (Uranus). But interwoven with these varied developmental processes is the human yearning for transcendence, for the peace that only comes from experiences best described as timeless, ecstatic, sacred, or mystical. These non-ordinary states are associated with Neptune.

Neptune is the planetary symbol of inspiration, that unexpected and inexplicable infusion of vision and creative insight that sometimes comes to writers, artists, musicians, entrepreneurs, or creative people from all walks of life. Our highest human attainments in the arts and sciences originate in the realm of intuition and imagination represented by Neptune. We cannot ignore its importance in human development.

Neptune symbolizes the expansion of our consciousness into dimensions beyond the mundane, material world — whether through the imagination, dreams, or religious experiences. It represents our longing for spiritual unfoldment toward the state of enlightenment or Self Realization. As a step toward that end Neptune usually induces a process of alchemy in which we feel ourselves dissolving. Often this is associated with a fear of losing control or a sense of having no boundaries. If we are able to overcome our fear of dissolution, the need to be somebody special may suddenly seem less important and may begin to fall away as we become aware of a great Light within us. Under the influence of Neptune, we transcend our thoughts, desires, and self-concepts, our minds become breathlessly serene, and we merge our very being into pure consciousness, the divine presence, eternal Being. As we learn to dwell in this vast inner silence, a radiant, formless, infinite awareness begins to manifest — the *Atman*, the Self. Neptune shows us glimpses of this state, which so many spiritual traditions teach us is the goal of our existence; a state in which we become aware that we are boundless and luminous, with access to intuition and inner vision.

Neptune is associated with exploration of the non-ordinary states of consciousness that have been studied most extensively by transpersonal psychologists. As writers such as Ken Wilber, Michael Murphy, and Frances Vaughan have shown, most Western psychological theories view the emergence of a mature, stable ego as the highest developmental stage attainable, ignoring huge regions of our potential human evolution.[52] Part of the mission of transpersonal psychology is to describe and understand experiences transcending ordinary ego awareness and space-time boundaries. According to Dr. Stanislav Grof, these transpersonal states include identification with other people, groups, or entire nations, even with other species or the biosphere itself; past life recall; memories of the history of the earth; memories of the lives of our parents or ancestors; kundalini awakening; communication with the deceased; ability to see auras; experiences of clairvoyance, telepathy, or other psychic phenomena; contact with animal spirits; channeling; UFO visitations; intuitive deciphering of universal symbols; and experiences of the Creator and of cosmic consciousness.[53] Neptune is the symbol of the fact that movement into the transpersonal realms described by mystics and seers is a natural part of our evolution, even if only a few consciously embrace this process.

Under the influence of Neptune we may be drawn toward the state of spiritual liberation, inner illumination, or union with God described in many mystical traditions. But Neptune can also manifest symptomatically as dependency disorders, difficulties coping with the material world, absorption in fantasies, delusions, and hallucinations, or peculiar ideation. While Neptune sometimes evokes periods of conscious spiritual expansion, in other instances it can reduce the person to a state of disorientation, helplessness, passivity, addiction, withdrawal, or inability to function. Counselors need to be prepared for the fact that at times clients will exhibit symptoms of an inexplicable weakness, devitalization, or loss of focus that is often directly correlated with transits or progressions involving Neptune.

Perhaps the classic example of such a process is the case of Carl Jung, who experienced a serious psychological and professional upheaval while transiting Neptune passed over his Descendant and natal Sun — the period he called his "confrontation with the collective unconscious." [54] Jung was flooded with visions, bizarre and often prophetic dreams, and psychic phenomena. His fantasy life became so active that he was compelled to withdraw for extended periods to his castle at Bollingen, Switzerland, where he gave his unconscious mind free rein through drawing, painting, dreamwork, mythological studies, and building with stones. He experienced visitations of an ancient Gnostic spiritual teacher named Philemon, and he penned a book called "Seven Sermons to the Dead" through a process of automatic writing.[55] While this was a tumultuous and confusing period in Jung's life, it was the time of his most important discoveries and insights.

Neptune and Locus of Control

To understand the developmental challenges associated with Neptune, it is helpful to consider Julian Rotter's concept of *locus of control*, which appears in two forms. An *external* locus of control is the belief that what is happening to us is governed by external forces. An *internal* locus of control is the belief that what is happening is governed by our own efforts and skills, indicating a feeling of control over events.

Our sense of locus of control greatly affects our behavior. People with an internal locus of control tend to get higher grades in school, take better care of themselves, and are generally more successful. Those with external locus of control are more prone to what psychologists call "learned helplessness," a construct that describes the plight of persons who are hopeless, passive, and unable to make effort to cope with their problems, even though they possess sufficient abilities and resources. Learned helplessness is the belief that nothing we do matters or helps our situation. It is closely associated with depression, which is often due to the feeling that we cannot influence circumstances. This is a Neptune problem. Neptune can paralyze our sense of motivation (Mars) and personal effectiveness (Saturn), often making us feel helpless and out of control. While Neptune passed over his natal Saturn, David (see Chapter Three) was unable to define social ambitions or to bear any responsibilities. During this period he was confused, uncertain about his direction, and unable to make decisions about a job or career path.

As I discussed in Chapter Four, many people associate astrology with an external locus of control, the view that our success and failure is due solely to fate and planetary influence, rather than to our own intelligence, talent, and efforts. But ultimately astrology teaches us to overcome learned helplessness and to develop a more internal locus of control. We learn that the planets are inside us, representing parts of ourselves, and that our own skills, intelligence, and actions affect the outcome of our confrontations with these planetary forces. We learn that the entire drama of development is taking place within our own psyches. Each planet evokes particular kinds of events and situations that challenge us to grow and change, enabling us to develop new awareness and to become more integrated. For example, through confrontations with external authority figures, we develop our own sense of discipline, structure, and responsibility (Saturn). Neptune's visitations reveal to us our living connection with the entire cosmos, the one consciousness that we share with stars, clouds, mountains, ducks, snakes, and deer. The developmental goal of Neptune is to awaken this expansive sense of communion with all life.

Neptune, Faith, and Self-Consecration

Through the influence of Neptune we come to recognize that there is a higher order, intelligence, or purpose directing our lives. We can call this the will of the Great Spirit, the unfolding of karma, or the Tao, the natural way of things. No matter what we call it, this realization awakens faith, a trust in life's unfolding. This attitude is known as surrender. While Neptune was opposite her Sun, a woman named Vicki became unable to focus on her clerical job and ultimately quit to dedicate herself to a new career as a spiritual healer and educator. Despite the precarious financial situation in which this choice placed her, she felt compelled to make this decision, as if commanded by a higher Law — the truth of her being. While it seemed to be a very impractical (Neptune) path to take, Vicki felt guided from within to pursue this work, which she felt would truly be of service to others.

During transits or progressions involving Neptune, what matters most is that we surrender ourselves deeply. In the state of confusion often associated with Neptune we do not know what is right, we feel unclear, and we are often unable to mobilize our will to act. However, if we learn to steady ourselves by developing a faith that is beyond the anxiety of our rational minds we may have the experience of consciously merging our will with the will of the universe. Often at such times we are aware that we are being swept along by invisible, mysterious forces much larger and more intelligent than ourselves. Over time we grow more willing to let go and trust the currents of our destiny. The oceanic tides of Neptune wash some things in our lives out to sea, into nothingness; yet in their wake everything is fresh and clean. We begin to trust the goodness of life and the grace and mysterious assistance we sometimes receive from unseen sources.

A woman with transiting Neptune conjunct her Descendant felt that her marriage was disintegrating, that she and her partner were drifting apart and avoiding (Neptune) true intimacy. She hung on through a period in which she thought of leaving her husband, but somehow her will was not strong enough to take this course of action. She only desired that whatever happen now be for the highest good of both of them and of all beings. In the midst of her state of uncertainty, she sat to meditate one day and had a clear vision that there was no fundamental difference between her husband and herself; they were, in essence, one being. She surrendered to the marriage, devoting herself to her husband, and they felt themselves begin to merge on the deepest levels of their seventeen-year marriage. They began to love each other more than ever before, and together they entered a state of ecstasy, Neptune's greatest gift.

Neptune's influence brings about a major change of personal commitment; for in the moment that we relinquish our egoic striving and desires, we begin to naturally dedicate our lives to service. Dane Rudhyar called this the act of "self-consecration to the whole," and considered it an essential turning point in the path of transpersonal living.[56]

I myself experienced this many years ago when I was living in a noisy, crowded, dirty city. One day, while transiting Saturn was exactly conjunct my natal Neptune, I walked the pavement searching for a job. At one point I cried out silently in prayer, "Let me do something with my life that will contribute to the healing of the Earth." In that instant, I felt a wave of bliss come over me, my prayer meeting with an immediate response of blessing from the universe. In such moments we experience a softening and turning of our hearts, which often leads to visions, dreams, and intuitions about how our lives and actions can be most helpful to all beings.

Many psychologists and therapists view the idea of surrender or self-consecration as an aberration, the sign of an exaggerated religiosity, a weakening of the ego, or an avoidance of the struggle to will ourselves into existence as individuals. In contrast, the astrological perspective is that there are stages in our development when we are ready to step beyond the struggle for survival, the quest for social status, the search for human love — times to taste states beyond form, beyond time, beyond ourselves. Neptune is a symbol of the fact that we can claim these others dimensions of our human inheritance, the vast potentials of mind and consciousness that most of us have not recognized before. Neptune teaches us the value of turning within and opening to the touch of Spirit, the descent of grace. Its lesson is that there is a depth of healing that only comes from journeying to the highest places of vision, from attunement to superconscious realms; and from awakening a peaceful, altruistic heart, filled with what Buddhists call *maitri*, or universal friendliness.

Plutonian Initiation and Transpersonal Growth

Neptune's lessons are only grasped when its activity is coordinated with that of Pluto. For to experience unity with the universe, we must first be tested to see if we can perceive our oneness even with our worst enemy. Pluto and Neptune operate as a pair, representing the two main facets of transpersonal development. If Neptune represents the revelation of the light, then Pluto is the revelation that comes from confronting the darker, hidden side of life. Neptune is the transpersonal ideal, the vision of unity, enlightenment, and universal compassion. Pluto is the ordeal that tests us in preparation for the transpersonal life, purifying us of self-centered intentions and motivations.

Neptune shows us glimpses of perfection and the awakening of more far-seeing ideals; yet Neptune leaves large corners of our personalities unseen and unperfected. Pluto counteracts the tendency of Neptune to be in denial, showing us the things that are inside us that hinder us from attaining our highest potentials. Pluto uncovers and eliminates the three poisons[58] of greed, hatred, and delusion, which obscure our natural clarity and openness — the serenity, vision, and universal concern that Neptune symbolizes. Pluto rules fixation; it shows us where our consciousness is fixated so that we can free ourselves. It may reveal our obsession with wealth or an object of desire; it may evoke possessive jealousy. By bringing this material into the light of consciousness, Pluto tries to bring about the refinement and upliftment of our character.

Isabel Hickey wrote that Pluto is the catalyst of a process by which the person becomes "the servant of the real Self and take[s] its proper place as a channel through which the power of the Essential Being can flow." [59] In her view, "Pluto is the death of the separated self." It teaches us "to die to the self and be born to a Self." It asks us "to be willing to be nothing on a personal level," to awaken humility, and to use our will appropriately. She observes that, "Every seed must be buried in the darkness of the Earth before it can break out of its shell and come up into light." Thus, Pluto's influence tends to bring extremes of light and dark: construction or destruction; illumination or obsession; wisdom or struggle. Hickey notes that it is often through painful experiences that we are able to grow into the light. [60]

I view Pluto as the planet of deep reintegration, metamorphosis, radical shifts in our consciousness, and experiences of rebirth. Its goal is self-mastery and increase in our personal power and effectiveness. When transiting Pluto opposed her Sun, a young woman left her parent's home for the first time to go to college and shed her old identity as a cynical, alienated teenager, becoming a hopeful, energetic woman with an active social life and well defined career goals. When transiting Pluto squared his natal Sun, a lawyer began to make more money than ever before and won a highly publicized case in which he faced down a corrupt lawyer on the opposing side. This latter example illustrates the fact that sometimes Pluto asks us to confront corruption or criminal activities.

In some instances, Pluto manifests in more extreme ways, through facing difficult circumstances. As I write these words (October 1995), transiting Mars and Pluto are conjunct. In the past week my house was burglarized, my neighbor's car was vandalized, another neighbor was robbed at gun point, and yet another was involved in an incident of domestic violence. A major forest fire has just devastated a large area of the beautiful park at Point Reyes in Marin County, California. These are not uncommon Plutonian events: crime, trauma, violation of personal boundaries, and destructive acts of nature. Also, my septic tank exploded all over my front yard; Pluto rules sewage, the return of the repressed, and the breakdown of all structures that are no longer working.

Developmentally, Pluto refers to the way the individual responds to the tragedies that are an inevitable feature of history and human existence. It rules bigotry and racism. Under the influence of Pluto we may experience historical events that are manifestations of ancient hatreds that sustain feuds spanning centuries — for example, the mutual animosity of some Jews and some Arabs, or the hatred that fuels the current war in Bosnia-Hercogovina. Pluto strongly influenced my father, who is one of the generation of soldiers that fought the battles of World War II, most of whom were born between 1915 and 1925 and had natal Pluto placed in the early degrees of Cancer. My father's Pluto was placed at 10° Cancer. In 1945, at the conclusion of the war, transiting Saturn was in early Cancer, passing over natal Pluto and that of his entire generation. His perspective was radically and irrevocably changed as the horrors and atrocities of Nazi genocide and mass incinerations were uncovered, and the world witnessed the devastating nuclear bombing of Japan. Through confrontations with cruelty and brutality, fascist politics, violence, and death itself, Pluto teaches us appreciation for our freedom and the preciousness of life. However, the situations often associated with Pluto are also capable of evoking lasting malice and mistrust, feelings that can become toxic to us if they aren't purged and relinquished.

Technically Pluto doesn't symbolize an individual stage of development. It is the symbol of our participation in an ongoing, all-human initiation in which we are faced with the choice between hatred and love; between seeking power and personal gain at the expense of others, or joining together with others in unity and shared commitment. Responding to Neptune we may wish to be selfless, loving, and forgiving. But when we meet the test of Pluto, we often face situations where it seems impossible to love and forgive, where it is easy to feel wounded and angry. Pluto's initiations often evoke such feelings in an attempt to raise us up from our animal nature, which reacts to life according to the law of the jungle: fight or flight, eat or be eaten, an eye for an eye. Pluto shows us the outcome of meeting life on these terms: mutual destruction, rage and despair, seething resentment, death in life. It offers us opportunities to learn to respond according to a higher law: Neptune's compassion, the ability to forgive.

Sometimes Pluto's tests involve painful events — deaths and bereavement, being mistreated by another, material setbacks, or loss of reputation. A woman with Pluto in the 2nd house in Cancer was swindled out of money in a real estate deal, when transiting Saturn opposed natal Pluto. A man named Richard with Pluto in his 4th house lost his whole family in the Holocaust. Richard underwent a lengthy struggle in which he came to grips with the pain of his losses. When transiting Pluto passed over the Ascendant of a man named Benjamin, seven of his closest friends and relatives died within a ten month period. Such Plutonian situations are part of our existence as humans. Although we may wish only for Neptunian light, visions, and inner journeys, Pluto's ordeals smash our egos ruthlessly. Often it is the wounds suffered through events like these, past or present, that occupy a client's attention.

George and Betty, a couple in their early forties, came to see me while George was undergoing chemotherapy treatment for cancer. Since they were born within a year of each other, they were both experiencing transiting Pluto in Scorpio square natal Pluto in Leo, and transiting Saturn in Aquarius opposite natal Pluto. George also had solar arc Pluto conjunct natal Saturn, and Betty's progressed Sun was square natal Pluto. George was fighting for his life and Betty was facing the possible loss of her husband. This was the first time something of this magnitude had happened to them. Neither of them had ever suffered a major illness or faced the death of anyone close to them. George began to see the futility of his strivings for power and status through his corporate career. He was filled with a sense of emptiness.

Their unexpected encounter with illness and possible death forced upon them a critical choice: sink into despair or completely reevaluate their lives. At first, both of them just wanted to ventilate all of their bitterness that life had dealt them such a cruel blow. However, the potential finality of the situation forced George to consider all the ways he had never truly lived fully. Several major changes resulted from this. First, George began to exercise regularly and enthusiastically. Then, he and Betty decided to go on an extended trip to Europe and another in Hawaii. They realized that they had to live *now*, while there was still time. They took up yoga and for the first time began to taste inner freedom. They healed some long-simmering disputes in their relationship that had been a source of discord and mistrust.

Mysteriously and miraculously, George's cancer went into remission — after the Pluto transits had passed. He had seen the face of death and its air of finality and this awakened him to the impermanence of life and the need to drink it to the fullest. His encounter with Pluto ended up catalyzing a profound experience of renewal. This story illustrates that while we may not understand the *cause* of such unfathomable events, we always have the power to respond with courage and to welcome the transformative possibilities of every crisis situation.

Another example of a Plutonian situation that lead to a positive transformation and empowerment is that of a woman named Gwendolyn, who had natal Pluto in the 10th house and transiting Pluto conjunct her Scorpio Sun. At this time, Gwen was pressured to accept a demotion during a hostile corporate takeover and major reorganization of her company — quite Plutonian events in themselves. Gwen fiercely fought the takeover, then ended up taking a position with a competing company that offered her a significant salary increase and greater job prestige. One of Pluto's tasks is to teach us, when necessary, to navigate skillfully in the world of power.

Through Pluto we gain an awareness of how power operates in society, especially through the agencies of government, banks, corporations and other influential interest groups. When the progressed Sun was opposite his natal Pluto in the 11th house, a man went through a transformation of his social perspective (11th house Pluto) as he participated in a class action lawsuit against a large corporation that had released toxic pollutants into the atmosphere. At first he became angry and cynical as he recognized that the corporation had no sense of social responsibility and would resort to all possible measures to avoid paying for their actions — even to the point of trying to destroy the reputation of key witnesses in the case. This situation led him into an enduring affiliation with an influential grassroots political organization (Pluto in 11th).

The misuses of power that we often face through the influence of Pluto are not limited only to such large-scale abuses, but may instead result from confrontations with the hurtful, wrongful actions of individuals — for example through experiences of betrayal. A dentist was reported to the state licensing Board by an employee after a casual conversation in which the dentist mentioned that he occasionally smoked marijuana; solar arc Mars was conjunct his natal Pluto. While transiting Pluto squared her natal Venus, a woman discovered that her boyfriend was sleeping with her best friend. A woman went to court after her husband beat her, when transiting Pluto passed over her Descendant. A man who stood to inherit a considerable amount of money from his mother was shocked when his uncle challenged her Will in court, leading to a protracted legal battle. Transiting Saturn was opposite his natal Pluto at the time.

The lesson of Pluto is that, as we witness some of the worst actions human beings are capable of committing, we are forced to recognize that these are our own shadows — that we, too, are capable of such actions. Through confronting situations like these, we see the hidden side our own personalities — our abusive or hurtful tendencies, our obsessions and compulsive behaviors. Pluto is the symbol of the deep personal growth that results from integrating this material. By facing our own unconscious in this way, not only do we become more self-aware; we also become less eager to demonize others and to see them as inherently inferior or inhuman — attitudes that are at the root of bigotry and violence in society. Pluto teaches us a fundamental lesson about the karmic law of action and reaction — that if we hurt others we ourselves are hurt. By showing us the effects of improper, unethical, or insensitive actions, Pluto strengthens our resolution to use our powers and capacities properly, reverently, free of the desire to do harm. Yet Pluto also shows us that we cannot afford to be naive, that sometimes we must fight for what is right.

A classic example of a Plutonian crisis is seen in the case of Doug and Patricia. Doug had been in business for many years. For some time he had worked in partnership with William, a man whose work habits were considerably different than his own. William took ten to twelve weeks of vacation every year, and worked part-time hours. Doug took no more than two weeks off every year and worked ten hour days, sometimes six days a week. Yet the two men evenly split the profits from their business. Eventually, Doug made the decision to stop dividing the proceeds equally, as William obviously did not do an equal share of work. Subsequently, William sold his half of the business. Now, six years later, William was suing Doug and his wife Patricia for fraud and embezzlement. He was trying to extract a large amount of money from them and was dragging them through a lengthy trial, in which Doug and Patricia were forced to submit for review all of their financial records for the past twenty years — a hellish ordeal. They felt they were being sued unjustly, and that William was trying to ruin their lives for no good reason other than greed and malice. They had already spent over $50,000 in lawyer's fees.

At the time, Patricia had transiting Uranus opposite her natal conjunction of Pluto and Moon in Cancer in her 7th house (open enemies). Patricia was in a turbulent emotional state (Moon), fearing that they were in danger of losing their home (Cancer) and all that they had worked for. This was an unprecedented marital crisis (7th house Pluto). Yet Patricia and Doug learned that, no matter what might happen with this lawsuit, they still had each other. Nothing except death itself could take away their love. They became more deeply committed to each other, sticking together through the toughest time of their lives.

Doug had transiting Pluto opposite his natal Venus in Taurus in Taurus in the 7th house. The lawsuit threatened their marital finances (Taurus, 7th house), and brought them into conflict over money with an old friend who had now become an adversary. In addition, Doug's natal Sun in Aries

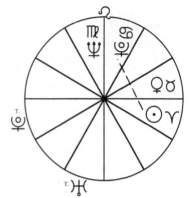

closely squared Pluto in Cancer, and both of these planets were being closely aspected by transiting Uranus in Capricorn. During this Uranus contact to Pluto, Doug was encountering an unscrupulous person who was trying to exploit his financial success. With Neptune near his Midheaven, Doug was a deeply spiritual man who did volunteer work with substance abusers and dying people. He did not understand what he had done to deserve this kind of terrible predicament. A devout Christian committed to love, compassion, and nonviolence, he struggled with the angry and vengeful feelings that were stirred inside of him by William's lawsuit.

While originally Patricia and Doug sought astrological counsel for predictions of the outcome of the lawsuit, I encouraged them to focus on trying to understand the *meaning* and *purpose* of these events as a form of spiritual initiation. Because of the Pluto transits they were both experiencing, I explained that they were being forced into a confrontation with the dark side of humanity, which in this case took the form of another person's desire to willingly injure them. The goal of this process, I felt, was for them to face evil without becoming evil themselves, and to defend themselves fiercely without succumbing to hatred. They knew they had ample justification for feeling bitter and resentful, yet they aspired to a higher ideal than to hate. They began to view their situation as a meeting with the collective shadow, which had meant the end of innocence yet could also yield deep wisdom.

Doug and Patricia scoured their souls, examined their own actions and motivations, and felt genuine remorse for past actions that were hurtful or unjust. They meant no harm to William and wished only to resolve their differences. Later they settled the case out of court, for a large but not devastating sum. They lost a great deal financially and in terms of emotional stress and drain of time and energy. But they had gained greater appreciation for their still good life and a deeper sense of closeness. Above all, they had been confronted with a situation that tested their capacity to love.

Pluto teaches us that our goal is not to dissolve into Neptunian ecstasy and mystical experience. Rather, its lesson is that, having perceived both a higher order of unity and the divisive effects of hatred, we can act in the world with the right motivation, free of the desire to control or injure others — powerful but not power hungry. Pluto confronts us with the violence and cruelty of both nature and humanity, in order that we become free of violence and cruelty. Pluto liberates us from these poisons so that we might become truly human.

As I alluded to earlier, this is not to deny that under some circumstances outrage can be healthy. In some instances Pluto challenges us to confront injustice and bring the truth into the light of day. The chart of the Dalai Lama[60] shows Pluto closely conjunct the Ascendant and south lunar node and widely conjunct the Sun. He has fought courageously against

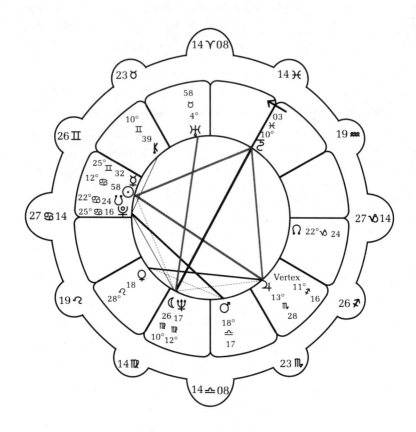

The Dalai Lama
7/6/1935, 6:00 AM TLT
GMT: 7/5/1935 at 11:15
Tangster, Tsinghai Province, Tibet
36N32 101E12
Source: Lois Rodden, *Astrodata II*

the Chinese invasion and occupation of Tibet since 1959, bringing human rights abuses (murder, rape, torture) and the destruction of temples and monasteries — monuments of a priceless cultural tradition — to the world's attention. Yet he has done so without advocating violence and without losing sight of the essential humanity of the Chinese — however wrong their actions and policies have been, and continue to be to this day. Reading his books and hearing his lectures, I am always amazed at how free of malice, bitterness, and hatred he is, even though his entire life has been dominated by the violent decimation and exile of his people.

The Dalai Lama also has Moon closely conjunct Neptune, symbolizing his great compassion, his selfless dedication to the service of his people, and his living embodiment of the ideal of Buddhahood. He is a religious teacher (Saturn in Pisces in 9th house), a political leader and activist (Uranus in 10th), and a monk dedicated to his spiritual practices (Sun in 12th). With Sun in a Grand Trine with Jupiter and the 9th house Saturn, he is a man of wisdom, moral strength, and spiritual authority. His life demonstrates how sometimes the worst of circumstances brings out the best in us. He exemplifies a higher level of psychological and spiritual development to which all of us can aspire.

Finally, let me note in passing that Pluto is sometimes associated with death-rebirth experiences, including passage through the perinatal states described by Stanislav Grof, one of the foremost researchers in the field of transpersonal psychology. Dr. Grof has extensively documented the process whereby an individual experientially relives four stages of biological birth and their corresponding psychological and emotional states.[62] In the first two of the "perinatal" stages the individual re-experiences the peace of the intrauterine state of unity with the mother and then the sense of suffocation, entrapment, and loss associated with the onset of labor and initial birth contractions. In the third perinatal stage, the individual experiences a surge of intense aggressive and sexual impulses and images corresponding to the fierce, violent struggle of the infant to pass through the birth canal. According to Grof, this is associated with a psychological state characterized by intense excitement, arousal, agony, and explosive, "volcanic ecstasy." In Grof's view, the fourth perinatal stage is an experience of conscious ego death and psychological rebirth that can propel the individual into extraordinary transpersonal states of consciousness — such as journeys into pure light, experiences of being in God's presence, hearing the voices of angelic choirs, identification with all human suffering, revelations about the universe, and visions of wrathful demons and divine beings. While I believe that Pluto governs the entire process of psychological death and rebirth, its influence seems to conform especially to the themes, symbolism, and fierce struggle of the third perinatal stage.[63] A person whom I know had the experience of consciously reliving his birth during a holotropic breathwork workshop led by Dr. Grof. Transiting Pluto was conjunct his Sun at the time.

Together, Neptune and Pluto introduce us to some of the most transformative stages of growth that can be addressed in psychotherapy. Understanding the principles represented by these two planets allows us to form a complete picture of human development, and to foster the emergence of its full, multidimensional possibilities.

PART III

Astrology and Spiritual Counseling

CHAPTER ELEVEN

Transpersonal Astrology and Spiritual Emergence Processes

Transpersonal astrology is a new field that is evolving to address the concerns of the growing number of people who are exploring contemplative, meditative practices, and experiencing transcendence of the ego, spiritual metamorphosis, and higher states of consciousness. In my earlier book, *Astrology and Spiritual Awakening,* I described some of the central features of transpersonal astrology and how it differs from other approaches to the celestial art. In this chapter I expand my thoughts on this subject and offer further case examples. I would like to begin by making some general comments about the meeting of astrology and the broader field of transpersonal psychology, which has emerged in the past twenty-five years to systematically investigate altered states of consciousness, mystical experiences, and the phenomenology of meditation and other contemplative disciplines.

Transpersonal psychology was born from the recognition that human beings have capacities for religious, transcendent, or ecstatic experiences that are little understood by conventional schools of psychology. As these non-ordinary states of consciousness were mapped out, some researchers began to investigate whether these states might have some relevance for the practice of psychotherapy, since many people today are searching for a spiritual redemption that traditional therapies do not provide. Transpersonal psychology has not only described the full range of human awareness but has also tried to demonstrate that accessing expanded states of consciousness can be a source of healing for some of our most persistent forms of suffering.[64] Thus, doctrines and practices deriving from ancient mystical, spiritual traditions have been introduced into modern psychological practice.

In bringing elements of religious and sacred traditions such as Buddhism, Sufism, Christianity, Yoga, and shamanism — considered anathema to many scientists — into the practice of psychotherapy, transpersonalists have crossed many conceptual, philosophical, and professional boundaries. Many traditional psychologists have found transpersonal theories and methodologies quite threatening and have raised vehement objections to the introduction of such practices as past-life regression, holotropic breathwork, meditation, or psychedelic therapy.[65] Despite this resistance, transpersonal psychologists have actively pursued research in these areas.

Yet these same researchers cringe at the mention of astrology, as if to consider this subject would be to cross the lines of credibility. Curiously, transpersonal psychologists will study channeling, past lives, kundalini, near-death experiences, spirit guides, and auras, but many of them distance themselves from astrology because they believe that to consider this subject would call their scientific integrity into question. But just as transpersonal psychologists engage in sensible, yet open-minded reflection on these subjects so, too, it is time for them to reexamine astrology and to recognize its great therapeutic and spiritual value.

Recently within transpersonal psychology there has been a growing interest in spiritual emergencies — also known as spiritual emergence situations — in which an individual experiences a physical, emotional, or psychological crisis attendant upon the transition into non-ordinary states of consciousness.[65] Spiritual emergence is often associated with phenomena such as spontaneous kundalini awakening, mystical states of ecstasy and rapture, perceptions of the oneness of all life, or extrasensory experiences such as telepathy or precognition. It may be accompanied by somatic changes and symptoms such as shaking, trembling, swaying, crying, or reliving of past physical traumas. It may also be associated with phenomena such as channeling, perinatal states, near death experiences, psychic healing, purported abduction by aliens, or visionary experiences following ingestion of psychoactive drugs. Increasing numbers of counselors and mental health professionals are now being trained in methods such as meditation, mandala drawing, hypnosis, and holotropic breathwork, which can be used to assist clients undergoing psychospiritual upheavals. I believe that astrology can be a useful adjunct to these methods and can help facilitate informed treatment of spiritual emergence situations that promotes their optimal resolution. Astrology helps us to reinterpret or reframe events in the light of celestial symbols — especially important in spiritual emergence situations where it is essential for individuals to understand the *meaning* of the transpersonal growth process they are undergoing and its *potential* outcome.

The Timing of Psychospiritual Upheavals

Transpersonal psychology describes the range of states of consciousness available to human beings, but it does not provide an *individualized map* of the process through which we may enter into these other modes of consciousness. In this regard, astrology can be particularly useful. The birth chart helps us understand the timing of events, for example the probable duration of a psychospiritual crisis. These are often correlated with transits or progressions involving Uranus, Neptune, and Pluto, or with activity involving planets in Pisces or the 12th house — the domains of the chart most associated with self-transcendence and inner expansion. If a person has an emphasis in these areas there is a stronger likelihood that counseling will need to address issues of spiritual emergence.

For example, a forty-eight-year-old woman named Susan, with natal Sun, Mercury, and Venus conjunct in Pisces and in the 12th house, has felt since childhood that she can't define who she is, because her essential identity *is* limitless Being, the source of all. No limited self-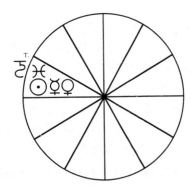

construct is adequate because her experience is that she is one with everything, everywhere. She has been meditating for a long time and she has traveled to many planes and dimensions in the invisible realms. This is not an experience that most people understand. Thus, Susan is quite private, some would even say reclusive; she stays focused inward, detached from external ambitions and rewards. Susan's path and only goal is to become a God-realized mystic, to seek oneness with the infinite Light, and to utilize her perceptions of inner worlds and her intuitive and psychic gifts to serve others.

In other instances a more situational crisis may arise. A person who by nature may be less spiritually oriented who begins to have a major Neptune transit may find himself or herself thrust suddenly into unfamiliar realms of perception. In such a case, a sudden awakening may occur that is not in line with one's prior constructs. After a lifetime of atheism, a seventy-two-year-old woman named Rebecca began to experience a relationship to God after several mystical experiences when transiting Neptune was conjunct her Ascendant. She experienced an infusion of peace and a golden luminosity filling her body and mind. She also had a number of vivid lucid dreams during this period.

Another example of a person experiencing a transition between states of consciousness is a woman named Barbara with transiting Neptune conjunct her natal Mars in Capricorn in the 9th house. Mars rules the physical musculature. Barbara began to experience strange symptoms — sensations of numbness, tingling, streams of energy coursing up her spine, fatigue, feeling paralyzed. She saw several doctors who thought she either had a neurological disorder, chronic fatigue syndrome, or multiple sclerosis. Understandably, these diagnoses caused her great fear and anxiety. Then Barbara had her chart done and began to examine the symbolism of transiting Neptune conjunct Mars; there was clearly a connection between the planetary symbols and her own experience. Neptune is associated with peculiar, non-ordinary states of consciousness, numbness, and perception of non-physical domains. Mars is associated with energetic phenomena, as well as with pain. She began to consider the possibility that what she was experiencing wasn't accidental. She decided to try to explore her internal sensations, rather than resisting the process or attributing it solely to illness. Now she began to view her symptoms as reflections of a process of awakening to flows of energy and perceptions of *prana, chi,* the subtle dimensions of the life force (Mars). A *chi kung* teacher taught her exercises for sensing energy flows, and she learned to channel healing energy through her hands. This transit was the gateway into a spiritual growth process for her. By helping her reframe her symptoms, astrology opened her to the realization that she was experiencing a meaningful unfolding, a spiritual emergence.

Of course, not all peculiar physical and mental phenomena are signs of mystical awakenings. Some of them are symptoms of real physical and mental illness; if a person suspects he or she is going crazy or exhibits unusual physical symptoms, he should be evaluated by an appropriate professional.

Identifying Current Developmental Issues

One of the ways astrology can be most useful for those experiencing spiritual emergence processes is its capacity to highlight the kinds of developmental issues a person may be experiencing at a given time. An astute astrologer can discern whether the individual is more likely to be coping with external tasks such as career development; or whether he or she may be engaged in the process of inward evolution toward mystical, transpersonal, expanded states of consciousness.

However, one of the things astrology has taught me is that evolution is not a linear process, with one stage neatly following the previous one. Instead, human growth usually seems to move unpredictably from one level to another and often proceeds on numerous levels simultaneously. As we have noted previously, human development is multi-dimensional, occurring on many levels concurrently. Rudhyar's observation that human consciousness and evolution is "polyphonic" means that we are evolving on multiple levels at once, signified by the interconnected activities of the planets. The process of transformation is very complex! In the old days we could go into an ashram, monastery, or temple and receive initiation, meditate, and be protected from the world. Under such conditions, with the proper training and sustained effort, we could presumably proceed directly toward the goal of enlightenment. But for most of us today, spirituality unfolds in the world, in the midst of demanding relationships, family ties, work commitments, artistic or creative pursuits, and strivings for achievement. Thus, we need an astrology that reflects the multidimensional nature of our evolution.

Astrology teaches us that there are times to step outside of time and to go beyond the world's objects, forms, institutions, and conflicts; and there are periods to come back down into time to be more effective within its realm. For example,

Susan (mentioned earlier), has transiting Saturn conjunct her natal Sun-Mercury-Venus in Pisces and the 12th house: She feels a deep pull to retreat. Her desire now is to work as little as possible, to spend time in seclusion away from her husband and friends, and to deeply interiorize her awareness. This is a period for her to explore the waters of spiritual growth and higher consciousness, through intensive dreamwork, meditation, and prayer.

In contrast, others may have had profound openings on spiritual or psychic levels but may now need to move "downward" along what transpersonal psychologist Ken Wilber calls "the spectrum of consciousness" [65] — in order to ground themselves, to complete unfinished business, or to express the energies of awakened consciousness through some creative project. The question is always what do we *do* with the experience of spiritual awakening: How do we express it? Even if we are expanding beyond individualistic self-preoccupation, we must still function as a centralized consciousness, as a Sun — a radiant, generative, creative light source.

Let's return to the example of Jim from Chapter Four (page 90). Jim had many spiritual, religious, visionary experiences in his youth, and then spent many years trying to recreate these "highs," fruitlessly. With Sun and Mercury conjunct in Aquarius in the 9th house and Jupiter in the 10th house, Jim had traveled widely to exotic lands and studied with many gurus. But he felt increasingly frustrated by the fact that he had never found his calling in life or settled down in a stable relationship. While he longed for God and enlightenment, he had not completed other, more pressing developmental tasks, such as finishing his education, developing a career, and finding a mate. Jim's consciousness was bound by these important desires, and he needed to address these issues before he could expand spiritually.

When Jim began psychotherapy, transiting Saturn was square his natal Moon-Mars conjunction in Scorpio in the 5th house. The Moon symbolizes feelings and memories, and quite spontaneously, Jim began to have powerful emotional catharses during his sessions, sobbing uncontrollably. The content of these sessions focused on his unhappy childhood and his family of origin. With natal Saturn-Neptune conjunct in Libra in his 4th house (family and emotions), the family was a lonely place for him, full of emotional distance, coldness, denial. Feelings were not spoken and there was an air of deep sadness in the household, due to a family tragedy during Jim's youth. Jim was now developmentally ready to spill his guts, to remember and grieve, and to contact a deep rage at his father. With Moon-Mars in the 5th house in Scorpio, he slept around quite freely. But underneath his sexually liberated exterior was a lonely man who masturbated compulsively. Although he'd spent years doing spiritual practices, fundamentally he was confused, troubled, angry, and had many concerns regarding his sexuality that needed to be resolved. With Neptune conjunct Saturn in the 4th house, before he could unfold his spirituality fully, he had to explore the garden of the family and of personal memory in order to resolve these emotional issues.

In Jim's case, the spiritual growth process involved emotional integration, recovery of submerged memories, and release of powerfully charged feelings. This made it possible for him to unfold his natal potentials, especially his intellectual capacities (Sun in 9th, Jupiter in 10th), which he'd never fully tapped. Jim reached a crucial threshold in his personal growth when, after signing up for an intensive weekend of spiritual practices designed to evoke expanded states of consciousness, he decided not to attend the workshop because he realized that "I don't need another amazing experience right now." Instead, he said, he needed to become more grounded and to improve his life in some more basic ways. As I noted previously, when transiting Saturn passed over his 9th house Sun-Mercury, Jim finished college and then worked toward his teaching credential. In this way, this mystically oriented and deeply thoughtful man was able to build a vehicle, a career, a personal life structure, through which he could live and embody his spirituality in the world.

In other cases, transits indicate a focus on spontaneous mystical experience. A woman named Kate had her natal Sun at 20° Capricorn in the 5th house. In 1993, while transiting Neptune and Uranus were conjunct her Sun, she began to have visions of the future and of past lives. She received inner guidance from great saints and spiritual masters of the past, and also began to channel information. Kate was being uplifted into an expanded state of consciousness. For a brief time she believed that she had been chosen by God for a unique spiritual mission. At one point she consulted with a psychiatrist, who thought she was experiencing hallucinations and delusions of grandeur. But Kate's work with astrology helped her understand the situation in a different light. Reflecting on the potent transit of Uranus-Neptune to her natal Sun, she understood that it was her time to receive an infusion of spiritual energy. She recognized that she needed to avoid the dangers of delusion and grandiosity; but neither did she wish to close the gates on these psychic perceptions and new spiritual insights. She dedicated herself to daily meditation practice and offered up prayers of gratitude for the gifts she was receiving. Later, with great humility and with a sense of humor about what she was undertaking, she began to teach others what she had learned through this spontaneous inner awakening. Her spiritual emergence was correlated directly with a planetary transit, which provided a clear symbolic indicator of such a process.

The journey of spiritual growth and psychotherapy is different for each person. Meditation, hypnosis, visualization, dream analysis, yoga — any of these methods may be appropriate for some persons at some times, and none of them are right for everyone. Rebirthing, holotropic breathwork, or past-life regression might be powerful therapies for some people and be totally unsuitable for others. One person may need to go to India to meditate, while someone else may need to start a business, or grow a garden, or have a baby. Not everyone will experience dramatic spiritual emergence crisis, kundalini awakening, or psychic opening. If our friends are experiencing florid visions of past lives or channeling ascended masters, we may wonder why nothing so dramatic is happening to us, but this doesn't mean we're missing out or are following the wrong path. Our spirituality may be unfolding perfectly in other ways. There are times when meditation is not likely to be efficacious, and there are times when concentrated meditation is essential. For Kate, with Neptune transiting her Sun, the time has come to do deep inner work. The tide of her being is flowing back to the source. Someone else might simply need to find a better job.

Coordinating Multiple Levels of Growth

As discussed earlier, we live within multiple narratives, multiple story lines reflecting the multidimensional nature of human transformation. It is rare to see a pure case of spiritual emergence unaffected by "lower level" concerns. Evolution is not a linear ascent of the spectrum of consciousness. It is a chaotic and seemingly random process — unless we know astrology, which helps us glimpse the secret intelligence of our evolution. Astrology reveals the polyphonic nature of transformation and helps us perceive how mystical or transpersonal experiences can be orchestrated into the larger process of biographical, personal development. The art of transpersonal growth is knowing how to coordinate exploration of spiritual emergence with other facets of our lives — such as issues pertaining to money, career, relationships, and creativity.

In spiritual emergence situations, one may experience states of consciousness that take one's awareness outside of time, beyond conventional boundaries, structures of time and space (Saturn) into formless, timeless realms (Neptune). But people in such situations always come back to earth and must orient themselves in the world of time. *Astrology always remains a tool for the temporal, embodied human being.* Its horizon is the "eon," the individual life cycle. It situates each event, including spiritual emergence, within that biographical perspective. From an astrological viewpoint, a spiritual emergence crisis is not an end in itself, but appears as one moment within the larger life cycle. What matters is the *meaning one derives from the experience,* and what the person does as a result of it. When working with a person passing through a psychospiritual crisis, I ask myself, how can this experience not only reveal unseen worlds but also transform the person's identity, actions, social involvement, or creative expression?

Reflection on the individual's birth chart *contextualizes* psychospiritual crisis periods and illuminates their direction and their goal. It reveals how the person is called upon to act as a unique expression of universal Being. On the transpersonal path our awareness may expand beyond our limitations; but the goal is always full embodiment, and the development of all our faculties and talents. The personality is the necessary vehicle through which a higher consciousness can flow into the world; thus, we work to refine it through a balanced approach to transpersonal counseling. Astrology is one important tool we can utilize to assist clients in integrating spiritual experiences into everyday activity, the grounding of extraordinary awakenings in specific, individualized projects.[66]

Broadening Our View of Spiritual Emergence

In addition to indicating the timing of psychospiritual crisis periods, astrology can also reorient and broaden our whole understanding of what spiritual emergence is. So many individuals that I work with as a counselor are grappling with spiritual growth issues, yet very few of them conform to the traditional image of the seeker of sacred truth absorbed in meditation, experiencing higher states of consciousness.

For example, a man from Portugal named Juan has a placement of the Sun in the 11th house at 20° Aries, conjunct Venus. At the age of twenty-five, while transiting Uranus and Neptune were squaring his natal Sun, he came to the realization that he was gay. This transformation of identity became the central focus of his life. The challenge he faced was how to express his true identity in a rather conservative, traditional, Catholic society that hasn't gone through the cultural changes and liberalization of attitudes regarding sexuality that have already occurred in countries such as the United States. For Juan to be free to be himself was not only an act of rebellion (Uranus) against cultural norms and religious prohibitions; it also required an act of self-dedication (Neptune). For he knew that there was going to be a terrible price to pay for his decision, and that, in a sense, he was offering himself up as a sacrifice. He felt a strong identification with the figure of Christ and his conscious acceptance of suffering.

During this transit to his Sun, the pressure built up for Juan to come out to his friends and family about his sexual orientation. This was a transpersonal act for him in that he knew he was taking a step that would impact not only his family, but also, to a small degree, his culture as a whole. Note that the 11th house (where his Sun was placed) is the domain of social awareness, our perception of the broader historical moment and our place in it. Juan's personal stand was an act of self-dedication to a larger cultural movement of liberation that would encourage everyone to be free to be whoever they are. At this time, Juan also experienced a non-ordinary state combining terror and excitement, crying, swaying, and inexplicable ecstasy. After he disclosed his secret, Juan reported a powerful release of tension, accompanied by trembling, exhilaration, and a feeling of divine protection and inner healing.

A man named Bill had the Sun in the 12th house at 25° Scorpio. While transiting Pluto was conjunct his Sun and while transiting Saturn in Aquarius squared his Sun, he was diag-

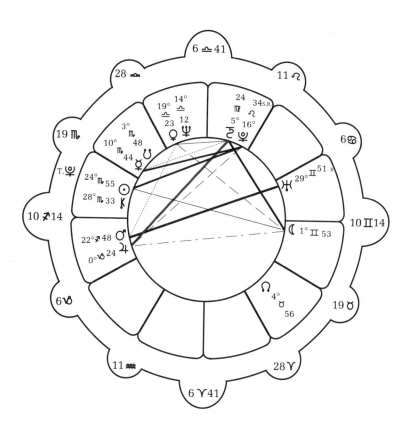

Bill
11/17/1948
8:30 AM
Paris, France

nosed with cancer. He has been a dedicated tantric Buddhist practitioner for many years. The 12th house is often, for those deliberately working on spiritual growth processes, a house of interiorization, of efforts to experience enlightenment, the pure Buddha Mind, the transcendent field of consciousness. Bill recognized that he had a choice: He could sink into feelings of victimization, self-pity, and hopelessness (some common 12th house themes), or he could transmute this confrontation with death (Pluto conjunct Scorpio Sun) into an occasion for self-transcendence — a higher expression of the 12th house. He went through an ego death experience, feeling that he totally surrendered to the way of the universe, the pattern of his karma. He accepted his predicament, became more fully dedicated to service (12th house), and was willing to let go of his personal identity — even his body if necessary. Bill deepened his commitment to be a healer in the world, through working with troubled adolescents in a hospital setting (12th house: institutions, and selfless service). A tremendous power began to arise in Bill through his meditation practices and also started to come through him in this work.

A predictive astrologer might have looked at Bill's transits and said, "It's going to be a really heavy time, a bad year. These are very inauspicious transits. You might even die." But such an interpretation would have missed the transformative potential of these transits and this life crisis. The way Bill interpreted his situation was that, through his cancer, he was confronting some ancestral karma. As we saw in the last chapter, Pluto is a transpersonal force, but what it represents is not the transcendent spiritual light of Neptune but the destructiveness and cruelty of humanity. Through this cancer, Bill felt that he was being given the chance to transform and release all of his hatred and aggression. "Something hideous grows within the minds and hearts of everyone," he said, "and it has taken form in my body now as this cancer. I could become angry and resentful toward my destiny," he told me, "but I prefer to try to use this situation as an opportunity to develop a universal heart, no matter what happens to my physical body." He transmuted the illness and became a contemporary Bodhisattva, a man of true heart and compassion.

Here a confrontation with death became the occasion for a spiritual emergence process, in which Bill worked to transcend his personal suffering by finding a deeper meaning in a crisis situation. His example demonstrates how it is possible to use any planetary placement or transit, however difficult it may seem, as a vehicle for conscious spiritual growth. Also, note once again how the awakening of higher human qualities of love, self-consecration, and universal friendliness are often linked to the Plutonian confrontation with death and the ultimate impermanence of life.

Bill's story also illustrates that the goal of the process of spiritual emergence is transpersonal activity,[67] in which the transformation of awareness promoted by contemplative disciplines and inner work are expressed in the world through an active life of service to humanity. Transpersonal activity doesn't mean going out on street corners and preaching that the world is coming to an end, or sitting on a throne and letting people bow to us slavishly. It means staying within whatever field of activity in which life places us and being a healer of our small portion of the universe. Each of us is asked to fulfill a particular function and to become the personal embodiment of universal archetypes, such as teacher, writer, mother, father, doctor, healer, dancer, artist, or civil servant. For example, Bill felt that his calling was to become the embodiment of the Medicine Buddha, striving to relieve suffering through his work with adolescents.[68] Our work is to embody this spiritual archetype with as great an attunement as possible to the highest potential of that ideal, as well as with humor and humility. We are not the archetype; we're just the vehicle for its expression.

Dane Rudhyar wrote a set of commentaries on a remarkable set of symbols known as the Sabian Symbols — which were originally published and popularized by philosopher and astrologer Marc Edmund Jones after they were channeled in a trance by psychic Elsie Wheeler in 1925. There are three hundred and sixty Sabian Symbols, one for each degree of the zodiac. The symbol for the sixth degree of Aquarius has particular relevance for our current discussion. It reads, "A masked figure performs ritualistic acts in a mystery play." Rudhyar's commentary states that this symbol refers to,

> the individual's involvement in long-established patterns of activity aiming at the release of collective power. . . . Rituals are binding, and often the performers wear masks, for they do not act as human persons but as focal points for the release of transpersonal forces. . . . The individual is seen having assumed a transpersonal responsibility. [69]

This highly significant passage provides us with a luminous image of transpersonal living as a *performance*, in which we put on a mask and perform our role, and thereby become an instrument for a transpersonal intelligence or power to express its intention. A careful study of astrology can reveal the nature of this role and teach us what tests we may face along the way. [72]

Pluto transits such as the one Bill experienced are extremely important in preparing us to become agents of transpersonal activity. Pluto often confronts us with our desire to control or to have power over others. We may have great power, insight, or talent, but if our need for admiration is too great, or if our seductiveness or sexuality is inappropriate, then we cannot be fully adequate instruments of Spirit. Pluto exposes these tendencies, humbling and purifying us so we can express power or insight in appropriate ways, through whatever task, activity, or field of life in which we are involved. For example, while transiting Pluto passed over the Ascendant of a well-known spiritual teacher, a scandal erupted in which his sexual escapades with numerous students were publicized. A similar scenario unfolded for another spiritual teacher while Pluto opposed his natal Sun. Ultimately, as we saw earlier, Pluto's intention is to transform our expression of our desires and our use of power so that our essential purity, goodness, and creativity can shine forth, unimpeded, unobscured.

The crises of spiritual emergence often prepare an individual to perform some needed role within the evolution of our society, humanity, and planet Earth. Although spiritual emergence is usually viewed in a wholly individualistic context, as the dramatic journey of the person into expanded states of consciousness, the individual's spiritual growth is in fact deeply related to collective evolution. In an era when our continuing survival depends on our capacity to develop more harmonious relationships with one another and with nature, it may be more appropriate to view each individual's awakening of self-transcending awareness as a contribution to humanity's spiritual awakening.

Astrology enables us to assist those who are stepping outside the conventional world view of our culture, for example, persons who are searching for alternatives to traditional work roles, or who are challenging gender stereotypes. But the birth chart is also a trustworthy compass for those who are venturing forth into regions where traditional therapists often become uneasy — regions beyond the ego, beyond exploration of the personality and its neuroses, beyond ordinary space and time boundaries. The correspondences we note between planetary symbolism (especially involving Uranus, Neptune, or Pluto) and spontaneous episodes of non-ordinary states of consciousness help us find ways to support, and cooperate with, these processes, rather than viewing them as symptoms of psychopathology. Just as we expect to focus on practical decisions and commitments during transits involving Saturn, so, too, when the outer planets are active, we are receptive to the possibility that material will emerge that defies traditional psychological conceptions — such as the perinatal and transpersonal phenomena that Grof and other researchers describe.[73] We begin to trust that such spiritual upheavals are initiated and directed from within by an inner intelligence, the Self, our innate urge to expand and move toward greater wholeness. Awareness of planetary symbolism helps us to assent to such a process, to have faith that this needs to happen now. The timeless wisdom of astrology can play a vital role in helping us guide ourselves and others through the many rites of passage of spiritual emergence.

Conclusion

In the twenty-first century, the use of astrology by psychotherapists will become commonplace. Astrology will take its
place alongside meditation, yoga, dreamwork, and breathwork as one of the primary tools of a transpersonal approach to
counseling. Therapists will utilize the birth chart to guide
others through the perplexing labyrinths and joyful discoveries
of the path of transformation, and to facilitate the emergence
of liberated men and women, who unfold all of their
capacities.

This book has tried to demonstrate the practical,
therapeutic applications of the birth chart. We have seen that
astrology is inclusive of all levels of our development. It helps
us to work with each person, wherever he or she might be in
life's journey. Whether the person desires more fulfillment in
relationships or needs to develop a sharper intellect, we are
able to offer focused guidance. Some may need meditative

silence, while for others we prescribe a solid dose of practicality. No developmental stage is higher or better than any other. We need each experience to grow.

In addition to reflection on the birth chart, a therapeutic astrologer uses the basic tools of psychotherapy: empathic listening, efforts to change the client's thinking and behavior, exploration of material arising from deep unconscious realms. We address all the major issues: sex, love, and money, work and family. We return to childhood memories and heart-breaks, and our most painful feelings. We uncover and conquer the demons we have feared. We put to rest the past and plot our future. Living in synchrony with the orderly movement of the planets, we begin to understand how skillfully we are carved by the hand of time.

In therapeutic astrology we work to liberate the personality from obstructions and to refine its expression. The birth chart, transits, and progressions illuminate the ground we need to cover to arrive at inner freedom, the blossoming of all we can become. The practical insights we gain from studying the birth chart help us gain fulfillment of our personal desires and our goals. And as we do so, we grow more open and receptive to a spiritual presence, a conscious intelligence within us that actively seeks to bring about our transformation. Wholeness, serenity, attunement to the inner light of consciousness, harmony in our relations with the world — these are the goals of therapeutic astrology. Like silent and compassionate gods, the planets point the way through each stage of our journey, awakening us to ever-expanding possibilities.

References

1 S. Grof, *Beyond the Brain* (Albany, NY: State University of New York Press, 1985), pp. 393–4

2 J. Hillman, Senex and Puer, in *The Puer Papers* (J. Hillman, Ed.) (Dallas, TX: Spring, 1979), p. 16.

3 C. G. Jung, A Study in the Process of Individuation, in *Mandala Symbolism* (Princeton, NJ: Bollingen, 1972; originally published in 1950), pp. 59–60.

4 For example, see G. Lewi, *Astrology for the Millions* (New York: Bantam, 1940); R. Hand, *Horoscope Symbols* (West Chester, PA: Whitford Press, 1981); D. George & D. Bloch, *Astrology for Yourself* (Berkeley, CA: Wingbow Press, 1987); S. Forrest, *The Inner Sky* (San Diego, CA: ACS, 1989); and *The Changing Sky* (San Diego, CA: ACS, 1989); S. Arroyo, *Manual of Chart Interpretation* (Sebastopol, CA: CRCS Publications, 1989); and *Astrology, Karma, and Transformation* (Sebastopol, CA: CRCS Publications, 1978).

5 D. Rudhyar, *Person Centered Astrology* (Santa Fe, NM: Aurora Press, 1976).

6 C. G. Jung, On Synchronicity. *Collected Works, Volume 8* (Princeton, NJ: Bollingen, 1951).

7 For this purpose, I regularly compare my horoscope with that of my client and note transits to both charts that might provide clues about the changing dynamics of our relationship.

8 For an in-depth discussion of aspects, see B. Tierney, *Dynamics of Aspect Analysis* (Sebastopol, CA: CRCS Publications, 1983). Also see S. Arroyo, *Astrology, Karma, and Transformation*, op cit., Chapter Six.

9 See N. Tyl, *The Expanded Present* (St. Paul, MN: Llewellyn Publications, 1976); and *Prediction in Astrology* (St. Paul, MN: Llewellyn Publications, 1991).

10 Note that all of these observations were made by examining transits and progressions involving only one natal planet, Neptune.

11 The researches of Michel Gauquelin and Cyril Fagan have shown that planets placed within ten to fifteen degrees (on either side) of the

Ascendant, Descendant, MC, or IC are accentuated and play a predominant role in shaping the individual's life and character.

[12] Z. Dobyns, *Expanding Astrology's Universe* (San Diego, CA: ACS Publications, 1982).

[13] Ibid.

[14] H. Kohut & E. Wolf, Disorders of the Self and Their Treatment. *International Journal of Psychoanalysis* (volume 59, 1978).

[15] See N. Tyl (Ed.), *How to Use Vocational Astrology for Success in the Workplace* (St. Paul, MN: Llewellyn, 1992).

[16] D. Rudhyar, *An Astrological Mandala* (New York: Vintage, 1973), pp. 379 ff.

[17] G. Bogart, The Use of Meditation in Psychotherapy: A Review of the Literature. *American Journal of Psychotherapy*, (volume 45, number 3, 1991).

[18] G. Bogart, *Finding Your Life's Calling: Spiritual Dimensions of Vocational Choice* (Berkeley, CA: Dawn Mountain Press, 1995), pp. 51–3.

[19] D. Rudhyar, *The Astrology of Transformation* (Wheaton, IL: Quest Books, 1980).

[20] G. Bogart, *Astrology and Spiritual Awakening* (Berkeley, CA: Dawn Mountain Press, 1994), Chapters Three and Four.

[21] Ibid., p. 89.

[22] This topic is discussed further in Chapter Eleven of this volume.

[23] *Astrology and Spiritual Awakening*, Chapter Three.

[24] *Finding Your Life's Calling*, pp. 51–3. Also see R. Moore, Ritual Process, Initiation, and Contemporary Religion, in M. Stein & R. L. Moore (Eds.), *Jung's Challenge to Contemporary Religion* (Wilmette, IL: Chiron Publications, 1987).

[25] A. Bharati, *The Tantric Tradition* (New York: Anchor Books, 1965).

[26] See *Astrology and Spiritual Awakening* for in-depth discussion of these issues.

[27] D. Rudhyar, *An Astrological Mandala* (New York: Vintage, 1973), p. 385.

[28] Personal communication.

29 Zipporah Dobyns, personal communication.

30 R. D. Stolorow & F. M. Lachmann, Transference: The Future of an Illusion. *The Annual of Psychoanalysis, volumes 12–13* (New York: International Universities Press, 1985).

31 R. Kegan, *The Evolving Self* (Cambridge, MA: Harvard University Press, 1982).

32 H. Kohut & E. Wolf, op cit.

33 Systematic presentation of the Sun's house and sign placement can be found in any good introductory astrology book. See footnote 4.

34 See the writings of Grant Lewi and Noel Tyl for clear descriptions of the various pairings of the Sun and Moon by sign placement.

35 The term "holding environment" was coined by British psychologist Donald Winnicott.

36 Personal communication.

37 Issues pertaining to Saturn and the father are discussed in Chapter Nine.

38 Parenting style has a major influence on development, especially the parent's style of imposing *discipline*. For example, power assertion (threats and punishment) and withdrawal of love are forms of external control, which may produce compliance in children. But discipline by induction — explaining why an act is wrong or violates a principle, or how it makes the other person feel — enables a child to absorb the parents' values and make them a part of his or her own standards and creates self-control. Studies have shown that authoritarian parents tend to produce children who are withdrawn, low in vitality, mediocre in social skills and cognitive skills. Permissive parents, on the other hand, produce kids who are vital and sunny but who have poor cognitive and social skills. However, parents who are authoritative, firmly governing but democratic, tend to produce kids who are self-assertive, independent, friendly, and high in social and cognitive skills. M Hunt, *The Story of Psychology* (New York: Doubleday, 1993), p. 372.

39 C. G. Jung, *Symbols of Transformation. Collected Works, Volume 5* (Princeton, NJ: Bollingen, 1956).

40 This section addresses some aspects of relationship analysis that have not been discussed by other authors; thus, I do not repeat material already

presented in books such as Stephen Arroyo's *Relationships and Life Cycles* (Sebastopol, CA: CRCS Publications, 1979), and Ronald Davison's *Synastry* (Santa Fe, NM: Aurora Press, 1983), both of which I recommend highly. My focus here is the individual's subjective experience of relationship, rather than techniques of chart comparison such as synastry, Composite charts and Time-Space Midpoint charts, and First Meeting charts.

41 For a discussion of the sexual profile in the horoscope, see N. Tyl, *Holistic Astrology* (McLean, VA: TAI Books, 1980), pp. 205 ff.

42 J. Piaget & B. Inhelder, *The Psychology of the Child* (New York: Basic Books, 1969).

43 L. Kohlberg, *Collected Papers on Moral Development and Moral Education* (Cambridge, MA: Center for Moral Education).

44 This is sometimes known as "good boy" morality. Think of how members of the Reagan administration such as Oliver North vehemently defended lying to Congress and the American public about their illegal activities in the Iran-Contra debacle (trading arms for hostages, supplying weapons to the Nicaraguan Contras) based on the argument that they were only doing their duty to protect the President and his policies.

45 J. Green, *Uranus: Freedom From the Known* (St. Paul, MN: Llewellyn Publications, 1988).

46 E. Erikson, *Identity: Youth and Crisis (New York: Norton, 1968).*

47 D. Levinson, *The Seasons of a Man's Life* (New York: Ballantine, 1978).

48 S. Arroyo, *Astrology, Karma, and Transformation*, op cit., Chapter Five; and A. Ruperti, *Cycles of Becoming* (Sebastopol, CA: CRCS Publications, 1978), Chapter Six.

49 D. Levinson, *The Seasons of a Man's Life* (New York: Ballantine, 1978).

50 R. Tarnas, *Prometheus The Awakener* (Oxford, England: Auriel Press, 1993).

51 A. Ruperti, *Cycles of Becoming* (Sebastopol, CA: CRCS Publications, 1978), p. 141–2.

[52] K. Wilber, *The Atman Project* (Wheaton, IL: Quest Books, 1980); F. Vaughan, *The Inward Arc* (Boston: Shambhala, 1986); M. Murphy, *The Future of the Body* (Los Angeles: Tarcher, 1992).

[53] S. Grof, *The Holotropic Mind* (San Francisco: Harper Collins, 1993).

[54] C. G. Jung, *Memories, Dreams, Reflections* (New York: Vintage Books, 1961), pp. 170 ff.

[55] S. Hoeller, *The Gnostic Jung and the Seven Sermons to the Dead* (Wheaton, IL: Quest Books, 1982).

[56] D. Rudhyar, *Beyond Individualism* (Wheaton, IL: Quest Books, 1979).

[57] The doctrine of the three poisons is a fundamental teaching of Buddhism.

[58] I. Hickey, *Astrology: A Cosmic Science* (2nd edition) (Sebastopol, CA: CRCS Publications, 1992), pp. 285, 287.

[59] Ibid., p. 292.

[60] The Dalai Lama's birth date and time are widely disputed. Lois Rodden (astrology's leading authority on the accuracy of birth data) uses data cited in a letter from the office of his Holiness, the Dalai Lama, and also cited in his Autobiography, *Freedom From Exile*. Other birth dates for the Dalai Lama that have been offered are July 6, 1933 and December 18, 1933. The birth data used here, July 6, 1935 at 6 AM, is from L. Rodden, *Astrodata II* (Tempe, AZ: American Federation of Astrologers, 1993).

[61] S. Grof, *The Holotropic Mind*, and *Beyond the Brain*, op cit.

[62] In a lecture given at the Cycles and Symbols Conference in San Francisco on July 28, 1990, Dr. Grof and his colleague Richard Tarnas reported correspondences between natal and transiting planets and the perinatal content evoked during sessions of deep, experiential psychotherapy. They associated the initial perinatal stage with Neptune, the second perinatal stage with Saturn, the third stage with Pluto, and the fourth with Uranus. Tarnas will discuss these findings more fully in his upcoming book, *Cosmos and Psyche*.

[63] F. Vaughan, *The Inward Arc* (Boston: Shambhala, 1985); and S. Grof, *The Holotropic Mind*, op cit.

[64] A. Ellis, Dangers of Transpersonal Psychology. *Journal of Counseling and Development* (number 67, 1989), pp. 336–7.

[65] C. Grof & S. Grof, *The Stormy Search for the Self* (Los Angeles: J. P. Tarcher, 1990).

[66] K. Wilber, *The Spectrum of Consciousness* (Wheaton, IL: Quest Books, 1977).

[67] See *Finding Your Life's Calling*.

[68] Discussed at length in *Finding Your Life's Calling*.

[69] Bill's story is recounted at greater length in *Finding Your Life's Calling*, pp. 118–120.

[70] D. Rudhyar, *An Astrological Mandala*, pp. 252–3.

[71] *Astrology and Spiritual Awakening*, Chapter Four.

[72] For example, See M. Murphy, *The Future of the Body*, op cit., and R. Woolger, *Other Livers, Other Selves* (New York: Bantam Books, 1988).

About the Author

Greg Bogart is a licensed Marriage, Family, and Child Counselor (MFCC) in private practice in Berkeley, California. He is certified as an astrological counselor by the National Council for Geocosmic Research (NCGR) and has taught and practiced astrology since 1981. Greg studied Comparative Religions at Wesleyan University, Counseling Psychology at the California Institute of Integral Studies, and received his doctorate in Psychology from Saybrook Institute. He teaches at the Institute of Transpersonal Psychology and at the Rosebridge Graduate Institute of Integrative Psychology. His writings have appeared in *The American Journal of Psychotherapy*, *The Journal of Humanistic Psychology*, *The Journal of Transpersonal Psychology*, *The California Therapist*, *The Journal of the Society for the Study of Dreams*, and *Yoga Journal*.

Greg currently resides in the hills of Wildcat Canyon, in Richmond, California. You can write to him c/o Dawn Mountain Press, P.O. Box 9563, Berkeley, CA 94709.

Also by Greg Bogart

Astrology and Spiritual Awakening

This book illuminates the stages of spiritual growth and awakening through astrological biographies of famous mystics, sages, lovers, and literary figures. Learn to utilize your own birth chart to find the most appropriate spiritual practice and to guide yourself on the path of transformation.

"A ground-breaking book. All students will profit from reading an astrologer whose insights are backed up by thorough research and balanced judgment."

Tim Lyons, Review in Planet Earth Magazine

"This is one of the best books in the field. Greg fills a vital need by moving deeply into the realm of spiritual astrology, making this normally difficult topic easily understandable to the reader."

Stuart Walker, Astrologer

"Brilliantly summarizes a transpersonal approach to astrology. What sets this book apart is its succinct and yet profound interpretation of astrological fundamentals."

Stephanie Austin, review in The Mountain Astrologer.

"Bogart follows neither Eastern mysticism nor Rudhyar unswervingly. He has his own unique ideas and is, in the end, a teacher in his own right."

Donna Van Toen, Astrologer

"Exceptionally straightforward. Well-done, fascinating, and highly recommended reading. I certainly hope there will be more books from Bogart to follow."

Ken Irving, Editor, American Astrology Magazine.

244 pages, $19.95. ISBN 0-9639068-3-6

Finding Your Life's Calling:
Spiritual Dimensions of Vocational Choice

Greg Bogart combines practical principles and lively case histories to teach readers how to find and fulfill their life's central work. The book begins by tracing the history of the concept of vocation in Eastern and Western religions. The author then discusses the varied ways in which a person can gain illumination of a calling — such as vision quests, dreams, and inner voice experiences. Bogart describes how an individual moves through the various stages of confirming and developing a life's work, and suggests ways to navigate the interpersonal struggles and internal conflicts that may be confronted along the way. This is not just another book about how to find a job, but rather a unique perspective on the search for a meaningful vocation.

"A rich theory of how one's calling can be an integrative experience combining individual self-actualization, social action, and spiritual concerns. You will find this book worthwhile if you are still searching for your true vocation, if you have found it and want to affirm it more deeply, or if you are engaged in helping others choose their callings. Highly recommended."
Tom Greening, Ph.D., Editor, Journal of Humanistic Psychology

"*Finding Your Life's Calling* makes a unique contribution to the field of vocational choice. It lucidly discusses religious, psychological, and spiritual issues involved in defining one's calling, including a transpersonal aspect that is usually overlooked. This excellent book opens up new perspectives in a venerable field of study."
Stanley Krippner, Ph.D., Author of Personal Mythology

"An important survey for anyone considering a career transition."
Diane Donovan, Bookwatch

176 pages, $14.95. ISBN 0-9639068-4-4

To order books from Dawn Mountain Press
Please use the form on the following page ➤

Order Form

Please send the following books. I understand that if I am not fully satisfied I may return them for a full refund, no questions asked.

_____

_____

_____

Name: _____

Address: _____

City: _____ **State:** _____ **Zip:** _____

Sales tax:
California residents please add 8.25%.

Shipping:
Book Rate: $2.00 for the first book and $1.00 for each additional book.
(Surface shipping may take three to four weeks).
Air Mail: $3.50 per book.

Send check or money order to:
Dawn Mountain Press
P.O. Box 9563-BBC, Berkeley, CA, 94709-0563.